THE ESSENTIAL ELEMENTS OF FAMILY-SCHOOL PARTNERSHIPS

A RESOURCE GUIDE FOR SCHOOL LEADERS AND TEACHERS

Denise Diaz Atwell, Ed.D.

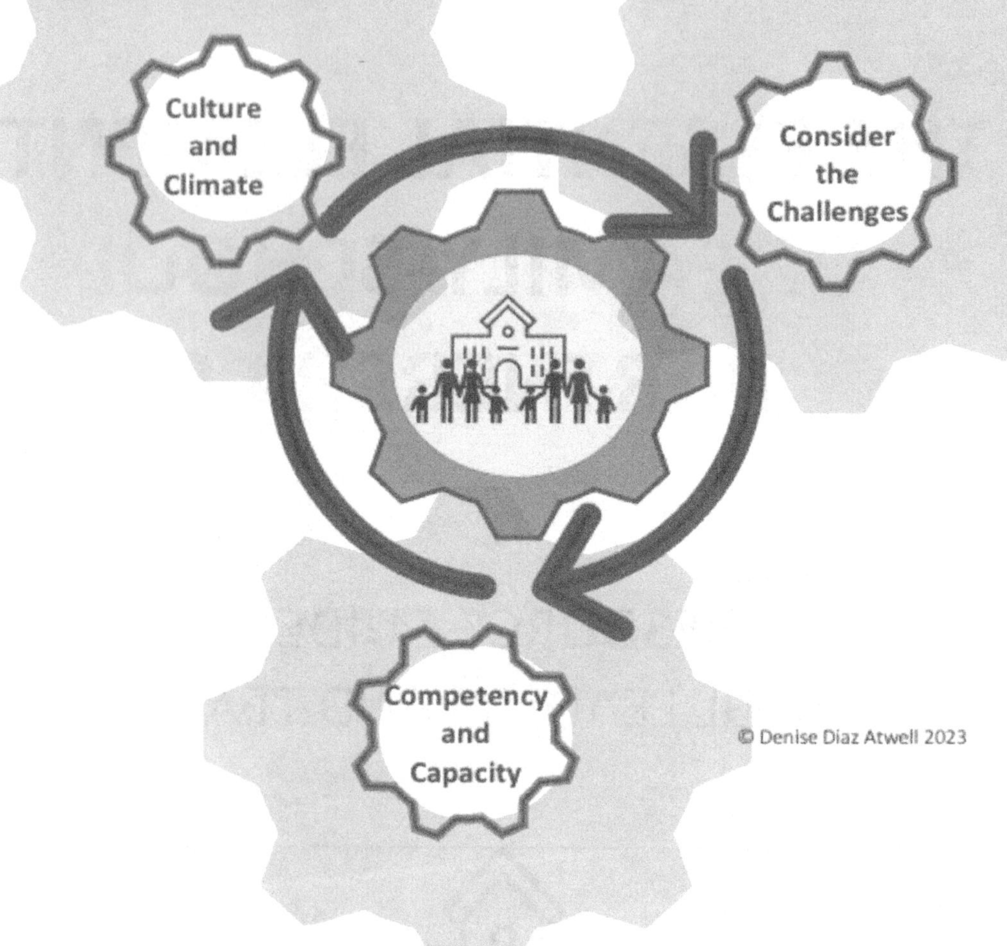

The Essential Elements of Family-School Partnerships

Published by KW Flash Publishing.
Library of Congress Control Number:
Paperback ISBN: 978-1-7374170-1-9

Dedication

This resource guide is dedicated to educators who believe family-school partnerships support student achievement and success! You can and do make the difference in the life of children.

Acknowledgments

A special thanks to those who helped make this book possible.

I give all the glory to God for giving me the strength and endurance to take on this project.

With my deepest love and appreciation to my husband, Everett, for encouraging me to write a book.

Thank you, Natalie M., Lori M., Shawn T., Jennifer G., and my mom Wilma, for reading my unedited book and giving me feedback on the content.

Special thanks to Scott A., my brother-in-law, AKA "Flash," who published my two books.

Thank you, Janell H., for editing my book, and Irene B., for designing the cover and formatting the content.

Education is the power to think clearly, the power to act well in the world's work, and the power to appreciate life.

— *Brigham Young*

Table of Contents

Preface

The information presented in this book comes from 30+ years of professional experience working to improve parent and family engagement in Title I schools. Along with field experience, knowledge of the subject, and doctoral research, "The Essential Elements for Family-School Partnerships" came to be.

Intended Audience

This book is written for an audience of school leaders, experienced classroom teachers, new or beginning teachers, and preservice teacher candidates or student interns.

Purpose

The book is a resource to enhance educators 'capacity for engaging parents and families in their children's education. This book aims to lead educators in establishing and sustaining family-school partnerships that support student achievement and success. The hope is that this resource book will become a valuable tool in an educator's professional toolbox.

Learner Outcomes

Using this book as a resource will offer an understanding of

- the benefits of family-school partnerships,
- the essential elements necessary for effective family-school partnerships,
- how to develop a partnership plan,
- how to collect and analyze data to identify the needs of staff and families and how to evaluate current practices to improve engagement efforts, and
- how to build the capacity of staff and families to support academic achievement.

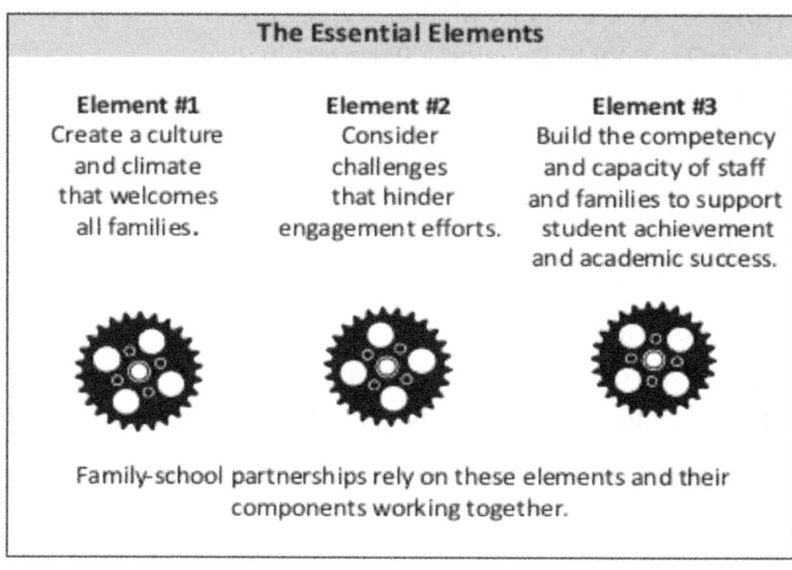

About the Book

The book's format is designed and organized into sections and presented in an easy-to-read format using bulleted points and matrices with suggestions, tips, and strategies.

Section 1—The Parts and Pieces—*Background*

Section 1 lays the foundation for parent and family engagement in education and why forming partnerships between the school and home is vital.

Section 2—The Gears – *Elements Essential to Partnerships*

Section 2 introduces the "essential elements" necessary for effective family-school partnerships. Chapters 3, 4, and 5 explain each element and its components and how they work together.

Section 3—Getting the Gears in Motion-*The Toolbox*

Section 3 was written to help schools and classroom teachers establish family-school partnerships and strengthen current efforts to engage families in their children's education. Chapter 6 offers step-by-step guidance on collecting and analyzing data relevant to the students and families and evaluating present parent and family engagement practices. Chapter 7 brings everything together with learning how to develop a "Partnership Plan" and plan relevant capacity-building activities for staff and families.

Written like an owner's manual, chapter 8 provides an overview of the essential elements (gears) in motion in a "how-to" format. Included in chapter 9 are example templates and additional resources and appendices. The templates are designed to aid in setting the gears in motion and correlate with the information in section 3. Additional information and resources included as appendices are for further learning.

How to use this book

1. **Learn about the "essential elements" of family-school partnerships.**
   - Read through Sections 1 and 2 to learn about parent and family engagement in education and the "essential elements" necessary for effective family-school partnerships.

2. **Collect and analyze data**
   - Read Section 3 to learn how to collect and analyze data relevant to evaluating current family engagement practices. This data will help discover what staff and families need to work as partners and identify barriers that hinder engagement efforts.

3. **Develop a "partnership plan" (for school or classroom)**
   - After collecting and analyzing data, follow the steps to developing a partnership plan for the school or classroom. Once a partnership plan is developed, begin planning, in detail, capacity-building activities.

Section 1
The Parts and Pieces

Background of the parts and pieces

Per Merriam-Webster, https://www.merriam-webster.com/dictionary/metaphor, a metaphor is an object, activity, or idea used to symbolize something else.

The representation of gears is used as a metaphor throughout this book to illustrate how family-school partnerships are like a working machine.

Gears are used in a variety of mechanical devices used in everyday life. Gears are wheels with teeth or cogs that fit together. Gears come in many shapes and sizes. Each gear works independently, but creating movement depends on gears turning in tandem to steer, change direction, or speed of motion.

Atwell's Essential Elements

The essential elements create meaningful partnerships between the home and school and families and school staff.

The essential elements are

- ***Culture and Climate*** - Address the culture and climate of the school and ensure the school environment has a communicated vision and mission for a family-school partnership, welcomes all families, and strives to build relationships between staff and families.
- ***Challenges and Conditions to Consider*** -To make the most of the efforts to engage parents and families in their children's education is to identify challenges that hinder engagement efforts. To identify challenges is to know the students and families served and recognize the needs and wants of staff, families, and students.
- ***Competence and Capacity Building*** - The purpose of family-school partnerships is for families and staff to collaborate to support student achievement and success. Accomplishing this goal requires building both staff and families 'competence and capacity by enhancing their abilities and providing them with the knowledge, skills, and resources needed to work as partners in supporting student academic achievement and success.

The Essential Elements of Family-School Partnerships

Effective family-school partnerships rely on the essential elements and their components working in tandem.

Essential Element #1: Culture and Climate

Create a culture and climate that welcomes families and makes them feel valued and respected.

The culture and climate are shaped by

- leadership support,
- a communicated mission and vision for family engagement,
- everyone working towards a common goal, supporting student achievement and success,
- time and effort invested in building trusting relationships with families,
- providing opportunities for families to come on campus or be engaged in their children's education, and
- effective communication between the home and school.

Essential Element #2: Consideration of Challenges

Challenges to effective family-school partnerships exist for staff, students, and families. Consider challenges that hinder engagement efforts by identifying barriers and looking for possible solutions.

To identify barriers:

- Know the students and families. Assess the needs of staff and families and find ways to meet those needs.
- Be familiar with challenges that stem from school and student demographics and population by reviewing data.

Barriers exist with the

- *school*
- *staff*
- *students*
- *families*

Common barriers are

- *language*
- *transportation*
- *childcare*
- *time or work schedules*

More difficult barriers stem from

- *poverty*
- *culture*
- *educational levels*

The most difficult barriers stem from

- *not feeling welcomed or valued*
- *lack of trust or confidence,*
- *beliefs, perceptions*

Essential Element #3: Building Capacity

Family-school partnerships rely on the collective capacity of both staff and families to support student achievement and success. Building capacity is improving or strengthening the organization and its people and their ability to fulfill the mission and vision. In this context, the mission and vision are building the capacity of staff and families to partner in supporting student achievement and success.

- ***To build staff's capacity*** *is to enhance their knowledge and skills to help families support their children's academic achievement by providing training, strategies, and resources to do so effectively.*
- ***To build families' capacity*** *is to enhance their knowledge and skillset to support their children's learning beyond the classroom, set educational goals, and ensure academic achievement and success.*

Addressing the essential elements helps

- create a welcoming culture and climate for all families,
- make building relationships among staff and student's families a priority,
- meet the needs of staff, students, and families when considering the challenges that hinder engagement and find solutions to overcome barriers,
- staff have a greater capacity to work in partnership with families in support of academic achievement and success,
- enhance families' ability to support their children's learning beyond the classroom, set education goals and
- work in partnership with the school to provide the best possible education for their children.

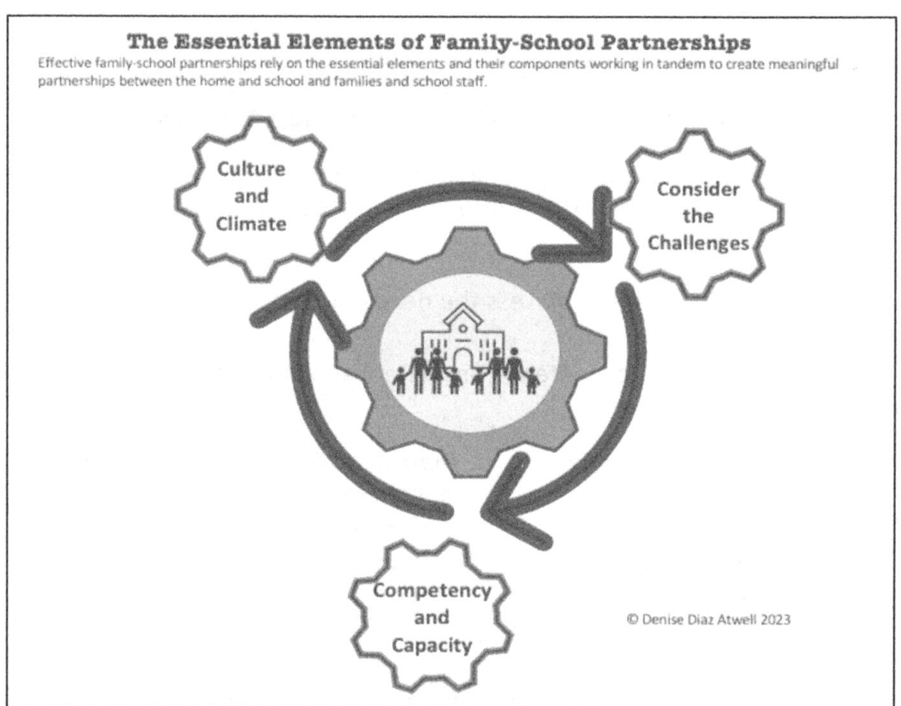

To establish and sustain partnerships follow these the steps. These steps are explained in Chapter 6.

Step #1 – Form a parent and family engagement team.
Step #2 – Write or revise your mission/vision for parent and family engagement.
Step #3 – Collect and review data.
Step #4 – Develop a partnership plan.
Step #5 – Share, implement, and monitor the plan for effectiveness.

What does a family-school partnership mean?

The term "parent" includes any legal guardian or parent in loco parentis legally responsible for a child's welfare. The family consists of grandparents, foster parents, friends, neighbors, and extended family members. However, today's average household is diverse and may include single-parent families, same-gender couples, mixed or blended families, and grandparents raising children. For this reason, the term "family" often replaces "parent" to encompass all persons involved in supporting a child's academic achievements and school success.

Parent and family engagement also referred to as family-school partnerships, are used synonymously throughout this guide, representing a shared responsibility among all stakeholders. The term "stakeholders" include persons committed to supporting a school and its students, including students, parents, community leaders, and educators. Community stakeholders are organizations, agencies, or businesses with a vested interest in the school. Therefore, a family-school partnership is everyone committed to supporting a school, and its students are working toward a common goal—supporting student achievement and success!

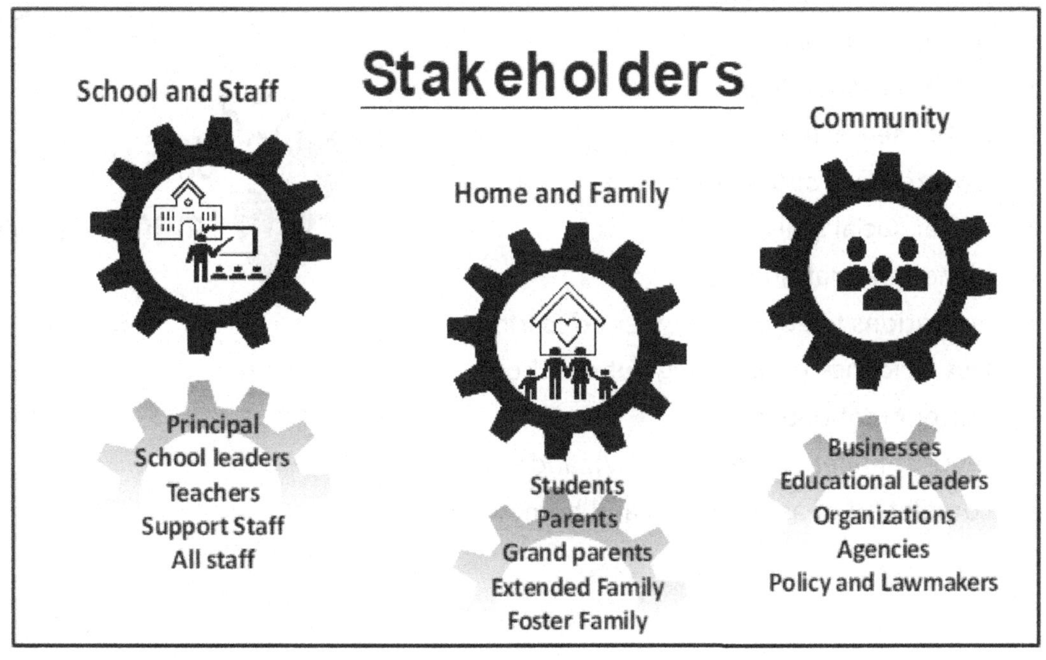

Who Benefits from Family-School Partnerships?

The indications from research are consistent in that there is a positive influence on children's achievement in school and throughout their life when their parents or family are engaged. Engaging parents and families in their children's education provide positive social, emotional, and academic results for children's well-being. Partnerships benefit everyone, especially children and schools, where all stakeholders share responsibility for children's academic success.

The benefits to students

Students have many benefits when their family partners with school staff in supporting their academic achievement and success.

The benefits to students may include

- a love for school and enjoying school,
- having better relationships with adults and liking their teachers,
- better performance in school,
- a passion for learning,
- increased student achievement,
- fewer discipline issues,
- more positive behaviors,
- better attendance,
- more self-discipline,
- higher self-esteem,
- a decrease in substance abuse,
- better social skills,
- higher graduation rates,
- aspirations to go on to higher education,
- less incidence of dropping out of school,
- better emotional health,
- more confidence (self-efficacy), and
- completion of assignments and homework.

The benefits to families

There are many benefits for parents and families when there is a partnership with the school and staff. Families, staff, and students reap the benefits when the school provides opportunities to build families' capacity to support their children's academic achievement and success.

The benefits for parents and families may include

- higher capacity to support their children's learning beyond the classroom,
- skills to engage in more discussions with their children about their learning,
- awareness about their children's social and emotional health,
- the ability to monitor their children's academic progress,
- more confidence in their parenting skills,
- the capability to set educational goals and aspirations for their children,
- feeling comfortable participating more in educational decision-making,
- higher capacity to advocate for their children's education,
- a better understanding of their children's curriculum and expectations,
- increased trust in the school and with staff,
- feeling more comfortable communicating with staff,
- having more positive perceptions of the school and staff,
- an increased understanding of state assessments and the ramifications of those assessments,
- awareness of educational laws and policies that affect their children's education,
- understanding promotion and retention requirements, and
- feeling valued and respected.

The home is the child's first school,

parents are children's first teachers,

and reading is the child's first subject!

Barbara Bush

The benefits to school staff

When the school and staff have the support of their students and families and when they form sustaining relationships, everyone benefits.

The benefits for schools and staff may include

- the capacity for staff to help families extend their child's learning beyond the classroom,
- beneficial relationships between teachers and their students and families,
- feeling respected as professionals,
- higher morale,
- higher job satisfaction,
- positive relationships with the support from parents and families,
- a better understanding of families 'cultures and unique circumstances,
- more appreciation for diversity,
- cultural awareness,
- additional support from the community and improvement of the school's reputation,
- fewer discipline issues and more positive behavior in students,
- amplified student academic achievement, motivation, and higher grades,
- increased communication with families,
- effective two-way communication,
- more constructive parent-teacher conferences,
- established trust between staff and families,
- Increased attendance at school events,
- additional participation and volunteer efforts from families, and
- background knowledge of their student's families and home life.

"The evidence is consistent, positive, and convincing: families have a major influence on their children's achievement in school and through life."

A New Wave of Evidence
— Anne Henderson & Karen Mapp

November is family engagement in education Month

In 1921, the National Education Association (NEA) created National Education Month in November to generate public support for education and raise awareness of the importance of education. Many educational organizations and school districts find ways to honor those who support a child's education by offering a variety of activities or events. The NEA recognizes the contributions of parents and families to schools across the nation, inviting parents to experience a day in their child's classroom. Visit the NEA website for more information: *https://www.nea.org/resource-library/american-education-week-november-15-19-2021*.

Interestingly, in November, Project Appleseed hosts a National Parent Engagement Month to encourage schools to raise awareness of parents 'critical roles in their children's education. For some examples of activities, go to *www.projectappleseed.org*.

Today, many states acknowledge the month of November as Family Engagement Month and encourage their school districts and schools to show their support and honor their student's parents and families. For example, the Florida Department of Education (FLDOE) provides school districts with a toolkit full of resources to help them celebrate and honor their students 'families during November. Access to their toolkit is available at *https://www.fldoe.org/schools/familycommunity/activitiesprograms/parentalinvolvement/family-engagement.stml.*

Taken from the FLDOE website,

November is Florida Family Engagement in Education Month, a time to celebrate the crucial role parents and families play in their children's education.

When schools work together with families to support learning, children are more motivated to succeed, not just in school, but throughout life.

The Florida Department of Education recognizes the vital role that schools, and families play throughout a child's educational journey.

DID you know? National Parent's Day is the third Sunday in July?

According to ***nationaltoday.com***, in 1994, President Bill Clinton signed a Congressional Resolution "recognizing, uplifting, and supporting the role of parents in bringing up their children.

Per ***parentsday.com***, "Americans recognize outstanding parents, celebrate the teamwork in raising children, and support the role of parental guidance in building a strong, stable society."

Chapter 2
The Law and Parent and Family Engagement

First and foremost, all children have the right to a free high-quality public education. A high-quality education includes a safe and nurturing learning environment with high expectations for academic achievement. Immigrant children and children with special needs and disabilities have additional rights to special instruction.

Through the Supreme Court, federal law has put some specific constitutional rights that protect parents and children. Although there is a United States Department of Education (US DOE) in Washington, DC, the responsibility of education primarily lies with the State Educational Agency (SEA) and districts—local educational agencies (LEAs)—unless it is part of federal law. Educators must understand and become familiar with educational law, especially the requirements and rights of the State Department of Education of residence or employment.

Some of the fundamental parental rights for public schools include

- school choices,
- a rigorous curriculum and up-to-date textbooks and technology,
- freedom of speech and religion,
- the choice to opt their children out of sexual health education and HIV/AIDS prevention education,
- the option not to have children participate in standardized testing,
- transparency around learning objectives and tests,
- the right to see all instructional materials, regardless of format or context (USC 20 1232(h)),
- information on school performance,
- parent-teacher communication,
- access to services and activities, irrespective of language or income,
- learning about evolution, not creationism or intelligent design,
- the right to opt children out of a classroom, and
- participation for student-athletes.

The Every Student Succeeds Act, ESSA (2015)

The Every Student Succeeds Act of 2015 (ESSA) replaced the No Child Left Behind Act. ESSA is a US law that governs K–12 public education policy.

ESSA ensures parents' and families' rights to

- parent-teacher conferences,
- reasonable access to staff,
- opportunities to volunteer and participate in their children's education,
- observe their child's classroom, and
- the right to ask for the qualifications of their children's teachers.

Title I, Part A of ESSA

Title I, Part A provides financial assistance to LEAs (local educational agencies) and schools with high numbers or high percentages of children from low-income families. Funding calculations use a formula that considers the federal poverty level and the number of students who qualify for free or reduced lunch or receive government financial assistance, each based on a per-pupil allocation determined by the US Department of Education.

Title I, Part A funding is the most far-reaching federal entitlement in public schools. By law, Title I, Part A funding must supplement, not supplant, efforts for raising the achievement of the lowest-achieving students through effective instruction, parent and family engagement, and professional development. Title I funds to ensure that all children meet challenging state academic standards.

Title I remains one of the most significant entitlement grants that benefit the most students nationwide. Many of the same children served under Title I, Part A are also served through other federal entitlement programs (i.e., migrant, ESOL, IDEA, etc.), each with additional parent and family engagement requirements (US DOE).

Source

U.S. Department of Education (website). https://www2.ed.gov/programs/titleiparta/index.html

Why mention Title I?

My personal work experience includes over 30 years in public education. More than 17 years were in or with Title I schools, specifically with Title I, Part A compliance requirements for parent and family engagement. ESSA's Title I, Part A, Section 1116 has explicit parent and family engagement requirements for schools receiving Title I, Part A funding. These compliance requirements directly influenced the research behind the essential elements and their components.

Best practices learned from Title I

ESSA's Section 1116 compliance requirements for parent and family engagement require practical, common-sense best practices that are a part of every school's parent and family engagement efforts. Title I schools are obligated to write or revise the PFEP and the compact annually, with parental input, and make them available to parents in a format and language they can understand.

The Title I Parent and Family Engagement Plan

Title I schools must write a yearly Parent and Family Engagement Plan (PFEP) and a school-parent compact. The PFEP outlines the school's plan to engage families in building family and staff capacity. Building capacity means enhancing knowledge and developing skills that promote effective school-family partnerships through resources or training.

The Title I Parent-School Compact

In addition to the PFEP, each Title I school will develop a school-parent compact. The compact is a separate document, an informal agreement outlining how parents, students, and school staff share the responsibility to improve student achievement. Below is an example of a compact.

<table>
<tr><th colspan="4">EXAMPLE –
Personalize to fit the needs of your school or classroom</th></tr>
<tr><td colspan="4">#1. Start with a goal or mission statement</td></tr>
<tr><td colspan="4">The staff, students, and families at _________will work together, as partners, to share in the responsibility of supporting the academic achievement and success of each student.</td></tr>
<tr><td rowspan="2">#2.
What or how can you accomplish your goal?</td><td colspan="3">#3.
Who is responsible? What will they do? Communicate these responsibilities with all stakeholders.</td></tr>
<tr><td>The staff will...</td><td>The student will...</td><td>The family will...</td></tr>
<tr><td>Learning environment</td><td></td><td></td><td></td></tr>
<tr><td>Curriculum/Instruction</td><td></td><td></td><td></td></tr>
<tr><td>Communication</td><td></td><td></td><td></td></tr>
<tr><td>Progress monitoring</td><td></td><td></td><td></td></tr>
<tr><td colspan="4">Consider adding a column for business and community partners.
By law, a compact must be developed with all stakeholders' input.</td></tr>
</table>

In addition to the plan and compact, below are compliance requirements per ESSA's Title I, Part A Section 1116.

These compliance requirements are embedded and woven into the "essential elements" and were significant to developing the "partnership plan" for this resource book because they are considered best practices that can and should be implemented in all schools.

Building capacity. Section 1116 (e) has 14 criteria for Title I schools to build capacity for involvement and support partnerships among the school, parents, and the community to improve academic achievement. Section 1116 (e)(2) allows schools to provide materials and training to help parents work with their children to improve their children's achievement, such as literacy training and technology.

Flexible dates and times. Section 1116 (c)(2) requires schools to offer a flexible number of meetings, such as meetings in the morning or evening.

Address barriers. Section 1116 (c)(2) allows the school to use its Title I funds to provide transportation, childcare, or home visits.

Monitor progress. Section 1116 (d)(2)(B). Schools must provide frequent reports to parents on their children's progress.

Conferences. Section 1116 (d)(2)(A). Elementary schools must hold a minimum of at least one face-to-face parent-teacher conference, and schools are required to discuss data with parents at these conferences.

Participation and involvement. Section 1116 (d)(2)(C) states that schools should offer families reasonable access to staff and opportunities to volunteer and participate in their child's class, including observation of classroom activities.

State standards. Section 1116 (e)(1). Schools shall help parents understand the state's academic content standards and standards for student academic achievement.

Language. Section 1116 (e)(5). Schools should ensure that information related to school and parent programs, meetings, and other activities is sent to the parents in a format and language that the parents can understand.

Parent involvement model (PI). Section 1116 (e)(11). Schools may adopt a PI model and implement model approaches to improving parental involvement.

Community involvement. Section 1116 (e). Schools may develop appropriate roles for community-based organizations and businesses in parent-involvement activities.

Source

US Department of Education. (2016). Amendment: ESEA/ESSA section 1118. https://www2.ed.gov/documents/essaact-of-1965.pdf

Section 2
The Essential Elements
~The Gears

Each of the three essential elements is explained in detail in this section. Chapter 3 is element #1, addressing the school's culture and climate. Chapter 4 is element #2, considering the challenges (barriers) that hinder engagement efforts, and in chapter 5, element #3 is building the competency and capacity of staff and families.

Family-school partnerships rely on a culture and climate that welcomes all families and invests time in building relationships between school staff, students, and families.

The climate and culture are the environment of the school campus and classrooms and the feeling one gets when they are in that environment and how they are treated. The school's environment is determined by the people in that environment and defined by those people's feelings, moods, perceptions, and beliefs.

A healthy school environment has a staff that invites families to come on campus, honors their presence, values their input, and encourages families' engagement in their children's education. Schools should seek opportunities for staff to engage with families to build relationships and form partnerships while working towards a common goal of providing the best possible education for the children.

Healthy and thriving school culture is shaped by factors such as

- supportive leadership,
- a shared mission and vision and the belief that parent and family engagement is essential,
- a clean and attractive campus appearance,
- the campus is family-friendly,
- providing opportunities for building relationships and forming partnerships.
- a staff that is welcoming to all families regardless of race, ethnicity, socio-economic status, culture, language, or education level,
- an atmosphere conducive to student learning, academic achievement, and overall success, and
- effective communication between the home and the school.

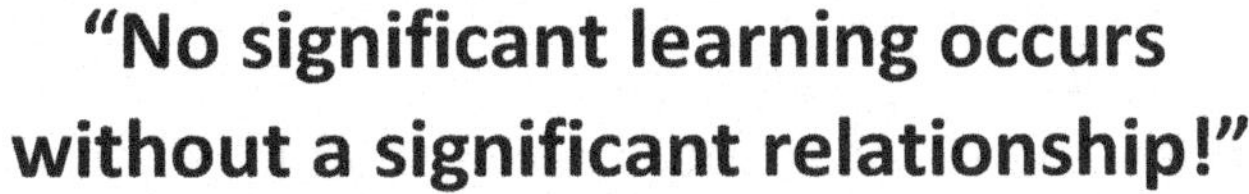

School choice

Showcase all the good things happening in the school!

Today, families can choose where their children go to public school. No longer are zoned or neighborhood schools the only choice for a student to get a public school education. Because families can choose, schools should market their schools and showcase what they offer to students and families. The parents and students are the customers! Make them want to be a part of your school.

The Elementary and Secondary Education Act ESEA, now ESSA, provides educational options for families that allow parents to choose other public schools or take advantage of free tutoring if their child attends a school that needs improvement or if their child's school is unsafe.

Parents are to be offered a range of school choices; however, these choices vary from state to state and school district. Each state department of education should be consulted about what their state offers parents. School choice provides families the opportunities to seek alternatives in public and private settings, such as magnets, public school charters, charter schools, private schools, and homeschooling.

Source

U. S. Department of Education (website). https://www2.ed.gov/parents/schools/choice/definitions.html

Who is responsible?

All stakeholders

The staff needs support from the home and family to provide the best possible education for each student and meet their learning needs. The school staff includes administrators, teachers, office workers, and support staff, including custodians, bus drivers, and lunchroom workers. Fundamentally, school improvement relies on all stakeholders sharing the responsibility of improving the school, including the support of businesses, community members, and faith-based organizations.

The school leader or principal

Family engagement is a fundamental part of school improvement. The responsibility for improving a school lies with the school leader, specifically, the principal. School improvement aims to provide the best possible education for students and ensure academic achievement and success.

Parent and family engagement is part of school improvement. Therefore, the school leader or the principal is responsible for engaging parents and families in their children's education. The goal of leadership should be to create family-school partnerships that support improving their school and ensuring student academic achievement and success.

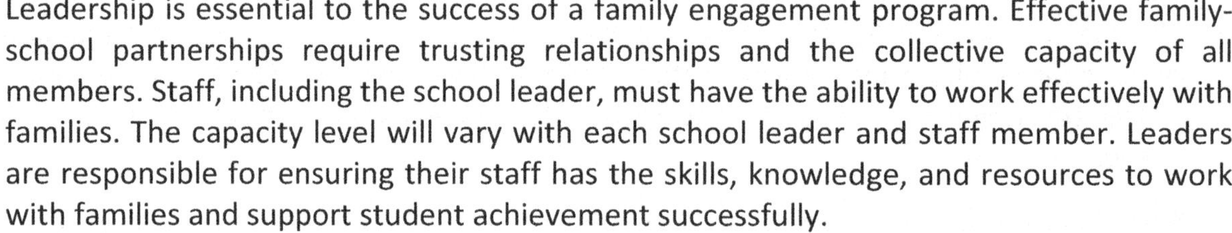

The school leader is responsible for

- bringing together all involved stakeholders,
- Initiating engagement efforts,
- establishing partnerships between the home and school, and
- building the capacity of staff and families to work in partnership.

Leadership is essential to the success of a family engagement program. Effective family-school partnerships require trusting relationships and the collective capacity of all members. Staff, including the school leader, must have the ability to work effectively with families. The capacity level will vary with each school leader and staff member. Leaders are responsible for ensuring their staff has the skills, knowledge, and resources to work with families and support student achievement successfully.

To maximize parent and family engagement efforts, the leader must

- communicate the importance of parent and family engagement with staff,
- have a shared mission and vision for partnerships,
- provide opportunities for staff and families to build relationships, and
- identify the needs of students and their families and find ways to meet those needs, individually or holistically,
- identify and address barriers that hinder engagement efforts,

- develop the capacity of staff to work effectively with parents as partners in support of children's academic success, and
- and enhance families' ability to support their child's learning beyond the classroom and support their academic success.

The following suggestions help the school leader initiate and lead change to improve parent and family engagement efforts.

Leaders should

- Ask for district support.
- Build their level of personal capacity for family engagement.
- Make family-school partnerships part of school improvement efforts.
- Assemble a family engagement team to spearhead efforts.
- Find out what staff needs to form alliances and offer building capacity opportunities.
- Reflect on current engagement practices and look for ways to improve.
- Develop a partnership plan to engage families.
- Create a mission and vision for engagement.
- Share expectations with all stakeholders.
- Provide opportunities for staff and families to engage and build relationships.
- Take time to listen to the concerns of staff and families.
- Build trusting relationships with staff and families with words and actions that convey the message that they are valued and respected.
- Take time to get to know the students and their families (background, home life, needs, etc.)

The classroom teacher

The principal plays an essential role in parent and family engagement in their school, but never forget that the first advocate of a student is the student's classroom teacher at school! The classroom teacher plays a vital role in building relationships with students and their families and has the most personal information about the unique needs of the students and their families.

Families

The family is a child's first teacher. To support school improvement, families should partner with the school and staff to support their children's education by attending and participating in school activities and events, communicating with their children's teachers, monitoring academic progress, setting educational goals, and extending learning beyond the classroom.

Have a shared mission and vision for engagement

A thriving school climate communicates a shared belief in the mission and vision for school staff and families to partner. All staff should foster family relationships and build rapport to support children's learning. Per the NationalPTA.org website, "Involvement does not just happen; it must be encouraged and cultivated with policies and programs that focus on what families, schools, and communities can do together to support student success." Students and their families remain a cornerstone of increasing student success and academic achievement in education.

The **mission statement** defines the task/purpose and describes what needs to be done, how it will be done, and for whom it will be done. The **vision statement** communicates what is to be accomplished (a goal) and how to achieve that goal (objectives). The vision and mission statements can be combined to be a purpose-driven statement that describes a common goal with a purpose and objectives to reach a result.

The USDOE mission statement per
https://www.ed.gov/parent-and-family-engagement/

"Raising the next generation is a shared responsibility. When families, communities, and schools work together, students are more successful, and the entire community benefits. For schools and districts across the U.S., family engagement is becoming an integral part of education reform efforts."

A parent and family engagement vision and mission statement should be a part of school improvement and drive efforts to increase student achievement and engage families in their children's education. The vision and mission statement should be developed with input from all stakeholders and communicated to all stakeholders. Consider making the vision and mission statement visible, incorporating it in take-home communication, posting it on the website, and if the school is Title I, including it in the parent and family engagement plan and school-parent compact.

- **Below are some suggestions for creating a mission/vision statement.**
  - Consider assembling a family engagement team to help create a mission/vision statement at the school level. IMPORTANT—get buy-in from all stakeholders!
  - Begin with a goal, a purpose for engaging families in their children's education, and forming a family-school partnership.
  - Turn that goal into a mission and vision statement for the school (or classroom).
  - Communicate this mission/vision with all stakeholders.

Source

National PTA (website). www.nationalpta.org U. S. Department of Education (website).
https://www.ed.gov/parent-and-family-engagement

Relationships are important

Successful family-school partnerships are built on relationships!

The number one priority in education is the welfare of children and providing them with the best education possible. Both staff and families want the same thing, for the children to succeed academically in a safe and healthy learning environment that helps every child reach their academic potential. However, neither the school nor the family can accomplish this goal alone. Educating children requires the support of many, the school, the home, and the community. For these reasons, family-school partnerships are vital and rely on relationships between the home and school. Students benefit greatly when their two worlds are bridged from both sides working in collaboration.

Provide opportunities for families

Building relationships with families begins with extending invitations to welcome families to visit the campus, participate and have a voice in their child's education, and engage with staff. Provide opportunities for staff and families to interact and engage. The relationships and interactions among staff, students, and families, heavily influence the culture and climate within the school and classrooms, creating a positive school environment conducive to student learning and success.

When there are relationships between staff and families and families feel welcomed in the school, there is an increased chance that families will partake in opportunities to build their capacity to support their children. Building families' capacity to support their child's learning is the goal of creating a partnership. Part of relationship building is getting to know the students and families and what they need or want from the school and staff.

Get to know the students and families by

- offering meet-and-greets,
- providing opportunities to engage with students and their families,
- talking with families, knowing them by name, and pronouncing their names correctly,
- finding out what they need and want by conducting surveys, seeking their input, or collecting personal inventories from families, and
- having team-building activities at school events.

Offer different types of opportunities

Different opportunities serve different purposes, and the opportunities offered to families should be designed to meet their needs and the needs of their children. Schools should offer a variety of ways for families to engage with school staff and their children's learning.

Opportunities can be classified as

1. **welcoming** (an opportunity for building relationships),
2. **academic, non-academic, and informational** (meetings and workshops),
3. **advocacy** (ways families can have a voice or be part of decision-making), and
4. **volunteering.**

Keep in mind that not all families can or will come on campus for various reasons, so find alternate ways to provide opportunities for these families. The opportunities provided to families should not be limited to face-to-face interactions. Schools can increase families' participation through virtual activities or activities at hosting off-campus locations.

#1. Welcoming activities

The most accessible opportunities begin by simply extending invitations and offering families the chance to come on campus and attend or participate in the fun. Attendance at "welcoming" activities is usually much higher than getting families to participate in academic and non-academic events or advocacy opportunities. Getting families to attend informational meetings or competency and capacity-building activities is a little more difficult but not impossible. It begins with building relationships and making families feel welcomed, valued, and respected.

Welcoming families serves the purpose of	***Examples:***
• helping families feel valued and respected, • building relationships, • and engages them with school staff.	• musicals, concerts, performances, and sporting events • art shows, book fairs, media nights, author conferences, festivals, and family game or movie nights • have lunch with their child

#2. Academic and non-academic activities

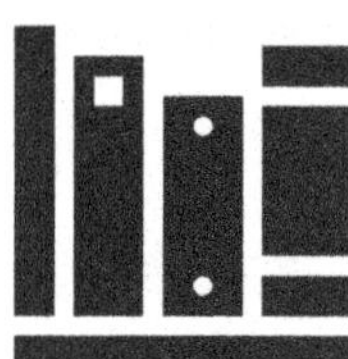

The goal of partnering with families is to support student learning and success. Schools must build families' capacity by offering academic and nonacademic workshops and training. Building families' abilities can be done by providing them with skills, knowledge, and resources that will enable them to extend and support their child's learning beyond the classroom.

The purpose of academic and informational activities is to help families

- support their children's academic achievement,
- help extend learning beyond the classroom,
- set educational goals,
- provide the best possible education for their children, and
- ensure their children are successful in school.

Some examples of academic topics:

- curriculum, standards, and expectations
- graduation, promotion, and retention meetings
- transitioning to kindergarten, middle or high school, or college and career
- testing and state assessment

Some examples of non-academic topics:

- behavior, bullying, or social or emotional development.
- technology, social media, and internet safety
- health and nutrition
- the transition from school to school

#3. Advocacy

To make parents and families true partners, schools can build families' capacity by helping them become advocates and giving them a voice in decision-making that affects their children's education. True partnerships are about sharing power and learning from one another.

Many schools do not encourage parents to be advocates or provide many opportunities to participate in a decision-making or leadership team. Schools should not shy away from promoting different or opposing points of view and encourage representation from a diverse group of family members that represent the interests of the school. There will be debates, compromises, and perhaps some opposition or conflict in the decision-making process. Schools must also reach out to all parents, especially those families who are hard to reach and engage.

School Advisory Councils

Most schools have a school advisory council (SAC) or leadership team. Most of the committee, at least 51%, should be composed of non-school employed persons, including parents, family members, and other stakeholders. Membership should represent the ethnic, racial, and economic community. Achieving balance with the membership requirements in schools that serve high numbers of low-income families is a more difficult challenge.

Parent-Teacher Organizations

PTA and PTO at the school level include members who advocate for supporting the school and students. PTAs are part of the National PTA, the oldest and largest child advocacy association in the United States.

Consider forming a family engagement team.

Ultimately, the school principal is responsible for everything that happens in the school. A family-school partnership starts with leadership placing importance on engaging families in their children's education. School principals have so much on their plates running the school, and often it is necessary to designate a person of leadership to delegate some of the responsibilities. For this reason, a school principal should consider selecting a leader to form a family engagement team, and the principal should have an active role as part of the team. The team must be representative of the school population and demographics. Having a team with a diverse group of members will provide broad representation and different perspectives that can help garner the support and buy-in needed to develop and implement a school-wide plan for partnerships!

TEAM = Together Everyone Achieves More!

Purpose of a family engagement team	Who should be on the team?
▪ conduct needs assessment. ▪ evaluate current practices. ▪ write and revise the partnership plan, Title I plan and compact. ▪ help implement, evaluate, and monitor these plans for effectiveness. **Tips** ▪ designate a leader. ▪ meet to monitor the implementation of the partnership plan. ▪ plan for meetings—set dates, prepare an agenda, have a sign-in sheet, and take minutes	▪ administration ▪ staff, teachers, and support personnel ▪ parents and family members ▪ community leaders and business partners ▪ make sure the team is diverse and representative of the student population. ▪ many schools use their School Advisory Council (SAC) because of the 51% parent membership requirement

Alone we can do so little.
Together we can do so much!
~Hellen Keller

Other Leadership Teams and Committees

Depending on the needs of the school there are many ways to offer parents a leadership role on a committee or team. Finds ways to include parents in the planning and decision-making that is taking place within the school.

#4. Volunteering

Provide ways for families to be involved or volunteer. School staff and teachers need and want parents and families to volunteer their time and talents to help in the classroom or school. Some parents cannot come into the school or classroom to volunteer but are willing to help in other ways. Consider offering "take-home tasks" for these families. Never forget to tap into human capital. Many parents have skills and talents that could benefit the school, classrooms, and students.

Below are some examples of ways families can volunteer

Inside the school or classroom	Outside the school or classroom or at home	Utilize families skills or talents
▪ tutor or mentor students ▪ assist in the classroom, lunchroom, media center, or car/bus line. ▪ help with school projects. ▪ participate in developing school plans ▪ serve on a committee. ▪ file, photocopy, sort mail ▪ prepare or deliver materials. ▪ read to students. ▪ helping in the front office ▪ answer the school phone	▪ help at sporting events. ▪ band booster ▪ PTA/PTO ▪ parent committees ▪ fundraising ▪ field trips ▪ newsletters ▪ updating social media ▪ organize events. ▪ run errands for the school. ▪ carpooling	▪ teach an after-school class or hobby. ▪ coach ▪ participate in academic events like science fairs, STEM programs, math contests. ▪ organize a literacy activity, such as an author visit. ▪ be a guest speaker. ▪ run a club

How to make the most of the opportunities

Below are proven strategies that will help make the most of every opportunity. First and foremost is to plan with attention to detail.

- **Invite** - Extend multiple invitations and personally invite families.
- **Advertise** dates and times of events. Send reminders.
- **Greet and welcome** families when they come on campus, making them glad they are there.
- **Encourage participation**. Communicate the importance, offer incentives, and find a hook to get them to attend.
- **Offer flexible scheduling** by varying dates and times or changing the format and location to offer activities off campus or in the families' community. Try offering some opportunities virtually.
- **Identify and address** barriers that hinder attendance.
- **Build relationships**! Offer informal meet and greets. Include a team-building activity at the start of events.

Always plan ahead

Families have busy work schedules. Most school planning occurs in the spring or summer before the start of the school year. Planning school events and activities allow schools to provide these dates to families at the beginning of the school year. Give families early dates to mark their calendars and plan around their busy schedules. Continue inviting families and finding creative ways to encourage attendance to visit the campus, attend events, and participate in activities. As dates of events and activities approach, families will need to be reminded and try using multiple forms of communication.

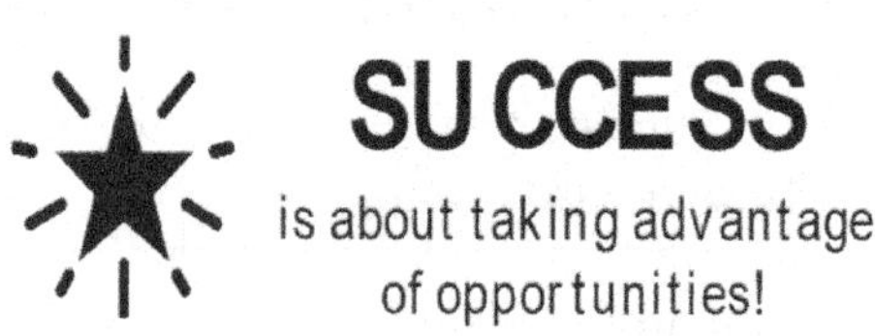

-Mike Ditka

SUCCESS
is 90% preparation and
only 10% perspiration.

-The great scientist Louis Pasteur

Be flexible with the schedule.

To maximize attendance and encourage participation in meetings and events, be flexible with scheduling—survey families for their preferred days, times, locations, and face-to-face or virtual.

Consider the following:

- For families with children in different grades or with siblings who attend a feeder school, try to schedule school events on other dates so there is no conflict for families.
- Coordinate dates around community events and holidays.
- Host activities during the day, in the evenings, or Saturdays to accommodate families' varying schedules and offer multiple dates and times.
- Offer opportunities in different formats like face-to-face, virtual, whole group, small group, hands-on, and make-and-take activities.
- Videotape or Record workshops or programs and allow families to watch them at their convenience.

Consider the reasons for low attendance or participation.

Families' busy schedules are the most common reason for low attendance at school events. However, in many lower-income schools, some common reasons families do not attend or participate include having no transportation, young siblings, no childcare, and non-English speaking/language.

Encourage attendance

For meetings, activities, and events held on campus, find ways to encourage attendance and make families feel welcome when they do attend. Consider serving food, providing incentives, or giving away door prizes.

Invite, invite, invite! Send invitations by

- using multiple methods of communication,
- utilizing technology and social media, and
- following the invitations with reminders in the families' native languages, as appropriate.

Here are some examples of barriers to low attendance and possible solutions

Consider possible barriers to low attendance and look for solutions.

time—busy schedules
- offer flexible scheduling.
- host different activities and events on other days and times (evenings, mornings, lunch, weekends)
- offer online meetings or stream meetings.
- videotape workshops and post them on the school website.

transportation
- use school buses with pick-up and drop-off locations for families in different neighborhoods.
- create or arrange a shared ride or carpool among families.
- provide access to public transportation and incur fares.
- host off-campus events.

food or refreshments
- provide meals or food if events are held during a mealtime.
- offer light refreshments.

language
- offer translation or interpreters for non-English-speaking families.

childcare
- provide childcare offer children's activities for siblings

Here are some suggestions for encouraging attendance.

Food

Offer food or light refreshments at the event, especially during mealtime.

Greeters

Have staff (including the principal) greet families when they arrive and thank them for coming when they leave!

Other Incentives

Offer other incentives to encourage attendance (try raffles, door prizes, give away a book, or game).

Here are examples of ways to invite or inform families of activities or events.

written
- flyers
- postcards
- labels in student planners

personal outreach
- phone calls
- personal invitation
- notes home

school/classroom
- website
- newsletters
- calendars
- callouts
- texts
- blogs
- podcasts

signage
- marquee
- front office
- car line
- bulletin board

community
- bulletins
- radio
- flyers
- local radio/tv station

student planners
- add personal notes.
- use stickers or labels with reminders

remember to
- send multiple invitations.
- use multiple formats.
- send reminders as dates draw near

Effective communication

In the school setting, most communication is usually heavily weighted on the school side, with information going from the school to the home.

For information that is sent to parents from the school, parents should...

- be aware of information that is sent home regularly, for example, weekly take-home folders, school calendars, newsletters, or progress reports,
- know that information is available on the website; and that the website is continually updated,
- know when report cards or mid-term interim reports go home, and
- understand how to navigate a parent portal to monitor their child's progress, grades, and attendance.

Two-way communication

Effective communication is meant to be shared (two-way) between more than one person or party. A conversation involves interactive dialogue or correspondence. Two-way communication is a conversation with two or more parties where each party can speak, listen, and be heard.

Is there two-way communication?

- Is there a way for parents to ask questions or share concerns?
- Are parents given access to staff via email, text, or phone calls?
- Do student planners allow for daily correspondence? Are parents required to review them nightly?

How can parents/families communicate with staff?

- email, text, phone
- website
- conferences
- student agenda planners

How can parents ask questions? Is there a process to share concerns or offer suggestions?

- a suggestion or comment box
- parents can text or email staff—including their child's teacher.
- blogs

Use multiple means to get information home to families.	
Calendars 	Families have busy schedules, and it is vital to give them dates ahead of time. ***Consider:*** ▪ timeline (yearly, monthly, or both), and sending reminders in newsletters, on the website, through call outs, and on the marquee
School or Classroom Website 	Keep websites or web pages updated and current with information. Consider the audience and make the website user-friendly and easy to navigate. ***Consider including the following, as applicable:*** ▪ tips and suggestions ▪ links to resources ▪ ways to volunteer. ▪ important dates ▪ policies and procedures
School Newsletter or Classroom Newsletter 	***Suggestions for a newsletter:*** ▪ keep it short and easy to read. ▪ provide it in multiple languages. ▪ make the newsletter available via the website, electronically, or mailed home. ▪ have a timeline for sending it home like monthly or weekly. Always include the school information, website address, and ways families can contact the school. ***Consider including:*** ▪ principal or teacher letter ▪ curriculum ▪ homework suggestions ▪ accolades and praises
Take Home Folders 	Some schools (mostly elementary level) have a weekly take-home folder. One side of the pocket folder contains student work, and the other has important information for the family. The folder is sent home on the same day each week, and parents know to look for the folder.

Communication through technology

Schools send home so much information to families, yet not all the information reaches families. For this reason, it is necessary to communicate in multiple ways, using various methods, and to find ways to ensure families know what is happening in school, know actual dates, and know where to find information. There are many ways to get information to families. Technology provides fast and efficient ways to send information to families via websites, social media, text messages, and callout systems. Email and texting offer teachers and students a way to have direct two-way communication. The use of technology is a valuable way to keep families engaged in their children's learning, even if families are not attending school events or on campus.

The 2019–20 COVID-19 pandemic necessitated immediate engagement and communication between the home and schools via different forms of technology. Not only did communication during the pandemic eliminate face-to-face interactions with parents, but the new normal for learning also relied on technology as teaching and learning were virtual during quarantine. Advances in available technology and its need during the pandemic raised the expectations of parents and schools as at-home learning requires parents to balance home and work with their children's homeschooling. The pandemic further made family-school partnerships even more of a priority as both the family and staff had to navigate learning new ways to support remote instruction through communication.

As technology evolves, newer and more efficient ways to communicate and connect with families offer educators more ways to engage families in their children's schooling.

Side Note: *The Department of Education approved ESSER, the Elementary and Secondary School Emergency Relief Fund, a federal program, as part of a larger COVID-19 aid plan. ESSER was established as part of the Coronavirus Aid, Relief, and Economic Security (CARES) Act in March 2020. The CARES Act provided direct funding to state education agencies (SEA) and local education agencies (LEA) to address the impact COVID-19 has had, and in certain contexts continues to have, on elementary and secondary schools.*

Source:*https://oese.ed.gov/offices/education-stabilization-fund/elementary-secondary-school-emergency-relief-fund*

Technology offers ways to

- deliver information,
- extend their children's learning outside the classroom,
- provide strategies to families to enhance their capacity to help their children at home,
- check to make sure homework and assignments are completed,
- monitor children's grades,
- exchange information,
- send messages,
- send flyers, invitations, and notifications,
- ask quick questions, and
- provide updates.

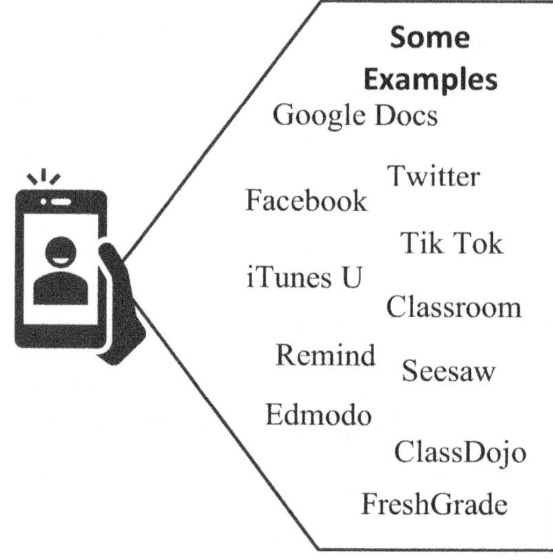

Be aware of child protection laws.

Family Educational Rights and Privacy Act (FERPA)

The Family Educational Rights and Privacy Act (FERPA) is a federal law enacted in 1974 that protects the privacy of student education records. FERPA applies to any public or private elementary, secondary, or post-secondary school and any state or local education agency that receives funds under an applicable program of the US Department of Education. FERPA gives parents or eligible students more control over their educational records and prohibits educational institutions from disclosing "personally identifiable information in education records" without the written consent of an eligible student or if the student is a minor, the student's parents (20 USCS § 1232g(b)). (An eligible student has reached age 18 or attends a school beyond the high school level).

Source

Family Educational Rights and Privacy Act. Retrieved from https://www.cdc.gov/phlp/publications/topic/ferpa.html

Children's Online Privacy Protection Act (COPPA)

Congress enacted the Children's Online Privacy Protection Act (COPPA) (15 USC 6501-6505) in 1998. It is enforced by the Federal Trade Commission (FTC). Parents have rights under COPPA for children under 13 who use a website or app to control the personal information collected online. The law applies to any vendors or operators of child-directed websites, including online services, web-based testing, and programs or applications that collect, use, or disclose children's personal information, whether at home or school."

Source

Federal Trade Commission. Complying with COPPA: Frequently asked questions. Retrieved from https://www.ftc.gov/tips-advice/business-center/guidance/complying-coppafrequently-asked-questions-0#A.%20General%20Questions

Protection of Pupil Rights Amendment (PPRA)

PPRA is a federal law that provides certain rights for parents of students regarding student participation in surveys, the inspection of instructional material, specific physical exams, and the collection, disclosure, and use of personal information for marketing purposes.

The requirements and rights of FERPA and PPRA came to light during the 2019–20 COVID-19 pandemic concerning the disclosure of personally identifiable information from students ' education records to outside entities when addressing the Coronavirus.

Source

U. S. Department of Education (website). Protecting Student Privacy. Retrieved from https://studentprivacy.ed.gov/faq/what-protection-pupil-rights-amendment-ppra

If you are aware of sending, using, or viewing child pornography online, contact your local law enforcement agency or the FBI if your child has received child pornography via the Internet.

Immediately report suspected online enticement or sexual exploitation of a child by contacting the National Center for Missing and Exploited Children at (800) 843-5678 or the FBI at **tips.fbi.gov** or file a report with report.cybertip.org.

Source: Nemours Kids Health. Internet Safety. https://kidshealth.org

Chapter 4

Element #2
Consider the Challenges that Hinder Engagement

Challenges to family engagement exist for the school, the home, the families, and educators. Because schools are diverse economically, racially, and culturally, challenges to engagement can vary school by school and family by family. Challenges become barriers in the form of obstacles, factors, or hurdles that hinder engagement efforts and can originate from families and school staff's beliefs, perceptions, and attitudes. Schools must know their students and families for school partnerships to be successful. School staff must be adept at identifying barriers and looking for ways to address the obstacles to maximize their engagement efforts.

Barriers are challenges in the form of obstacles, factors, or hurdles that hinder engagement efforts.	
	• **Obstacles**—perceptions, beliefs, misconceptions, and attitudes • **Factors**—poverty, language, educational level, race, student age, or grade level • **Hurdles**—transportation, work schedules, childcare, and language

Identify the barriers that hinder engagement efforts. Address barriers by finding possible solutions to overcome barriers.				
Barriers exist for the	**school** 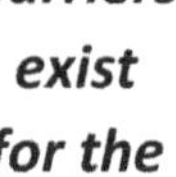	**staff** 	**student**  	**family** 

To identify and address barriers

- get to know the students and families,
- learn about the needs of staff, students, and families, and
- collect and review data.

Review school data

School staff must invest time and effort into getting to know students and families personally. To identify the needs of students and families, schools must invest time in building relationships and reviewing school and student data.

Look at the student population and school demographics.

School location
Where is the school located?
Are there safety concerns in the neighborhood or community?

Poverty
What is the poverty level of the school?
How many students receive free or reduced lunch or government assistance?

Student population
What is the breakdown in the student population?

- subgroups
- age/grade
- gender
- race
- ELL, SWD
- F/RL

Family dynamics

- education level
- careers, work
- home language
- culture
- parents/caregivers
- married/divorced
- foster care, adoption
- same-sex couples
- grandparents or extended families

Staff demographics
Is the makeup of school staff representative of the student population?

What you do has a more significant impact than what you say!"

Identify what students, families, and staff need.

As humans, we all have basic needs. Most humans want to feel needed, wanted, loved, respected, and heard. The educational setting is no different. School improvement goals must begin with assessing the culture and climate of the school and remembering the most basic needs of their human capital. The culture and climate of a school start with an environment conducive to building relationships and meeting the needs of the staff, students, and families.

Students need:

- the support from their families
- to feel safe
- to know they are cared for at school.
- to do well academically
- to fit in with their peers socially

Teachers need:

- to feel valued and respected
- leadership support
- collaboration and comradery with peers
- support from families
- well-behaved students
- their students to succeed academically

Families need:

- to feel valued and respected
- to know what is expected of their children
- to know how their children are doing in school
- the school to care about their children
- to feel their children are safe at school
- to know their children like school and do well in school
- the ability to communicate with the school and know what is happening

Administration needs:

- higher student achievement
- supportive families
- happy staff
- highly qualified staff
- well-behaved students
- supportive staff and district leadership

#3: Identify challenges that hinder family engagement efforts

"The challenge for families is that many have not been exposed to strong examples of family engagement. Some families may not feel invited to contribute to their children's education or feel disrespected, unheard, and unvalued. There is a lack of trust for some families due to negative past experiences with schools or educators." (Mapp & Bergman, 2019).

The most common family barriers are busy work schedules, childcare needs, transportation, language, or a lack of technology. More difficult barriers stem from poverty, culture, educational levels, or the makeup of the school demographics and student population. The most challenging obstacles to address are those that deal with feelings and beliefs, such as a lack of trust, not feeling welcomed or valued, or the belief that the school is solely responsible for a child's education.

Source

Mapp, K. L. & Bergman, E. (2019). Dual capacity-building framework for family-school partnerships (Version 2). SEDL. www.dualcapacity.org

Student/child barriers

Challenges may develop in forming partnerships between families and teachers and create conflict when there are problems with a child due to behavior or discipline problems. Similarly, problems can arise when parents feel their child's needs are not being met due to learning difficulties or the child is advanced and not being challenged.

A child's age or grade level can be a barrier because parental attendance and involvement typically decline as students get older. Data show lower levels of participation for middle and high school-age children than in elementary school. As children grow and develop, they seek more independence from their parents, but in reality, they need and want continued support from their families.

Adolescence is the transition years when a child matures into an adult and brings a new set of dynamics—developmentally, emotionally, and socially on top of academic challenges. Adolescence is when children learn to be independent but can be easily influenced by their peers. At the same time, parents are learning to gradually release some dependence while maintaining control. Often, adolescents begin to test boundaries and push limits, including experimenting with sex and drugs. During adolescence, the body undergoes physical changes, and some children develop an unhealthy body image. The physical and emotional changes adolescents experience create emotional highs and lows and may cause stress or depression. Children with strong family ties tend to move through this time of growth easier, knowing they have the support of their families. In contrast, those who do not have a support system are more likely to engage in risky behaviors which can carry over into school and academics.

> **"There are only two lasting bequests we can hope to give our children. One of these is roots... the other, wings."**
>
> Henry Ward Beecher

Families may need the support of the school to help them understand children's growth and development academically, emotionally, and socially. Schools can look for ways to build families' capacity by offering strategies and tips that help families navigate their child's growth and development and encourage their independence. Secondary schools have an opportunity to help bridge this difficult growing and learning curve and have the task of finding ways to keep families engaged with their children's education while not infringing on their need for independence. In secondary education, the school and families must be attuned to students' emotional and social needs on top of academic struggles that may increase the likelihood of dropping out.

Students with special needs

Individuals with Disabilities Education Act (IDEA)

The Individuals with Disabilities Education Act (IDEA) is a law that makes available free, appropriate public education to eligible children with disabilities throughout the nation. IDEA ensures that all children with disabilities have available special education and related services designed to meet the unique needs that prepare them for further education, employment, and independent living.

Parents have the legal right to have their child's educational needs professionally evaluated, determined, and served.

- Children and youth ages three through 21 may receive special education and related services under IDEA Part B.
- Infants and toddlers from birth to age two with disabilities may receive early intervention services under IDEA Part C.

IEP or 504

The law requires that K–12 students challenged with learning, emotional, mental, or physical disabilities be offered an IEP or a Section 504 plan. The IEP or Section 504 aims to provide the school and staff guidance in offering modifications or accommodations to meet the student's educational needs. Parent input and a parent's signature or permission must approve and implement either plan.

Accommodations/modifications

The student's needs can be met through accommodations in a general education classroom with assistance from a resource specialist (complete inclusion) or in a smaller class of students requiring individualized or small-group instruction.

- **Accommodations –** are not changes to educational content but rather ways to help students learn and process content. Accommodations should not alter the standards of what students are expected to know. For example, accommodation is a way to help students understand the same content but differently.

- **Modifications –** are changes in the educational content of what is being taught or what is expected of the student to learn. Modifications do alter the standards of what students are expected to know.

Response to Intervention (RTI)

Before a child is referred to special education services, part of the evaluation and assessment process is documenting interventions to help the child. Many schools refer to this as RTI, a response to intervention. RTI is a design of levels or tiers of teaching and learning strategies that increase intensity and support.

Positive Behavior Support (PBS)

PBS or PBIS (Positive Behavioral Interventions and Supports) is a set of research-based strategies to decrease problem behaviors by using an approach for improving the behavior of all children by raising their levels of social competence. PBS or PBIS integrates research-based practices and interventions with a more preventive and positive approach that reduces problem behaviors and enhances learning.

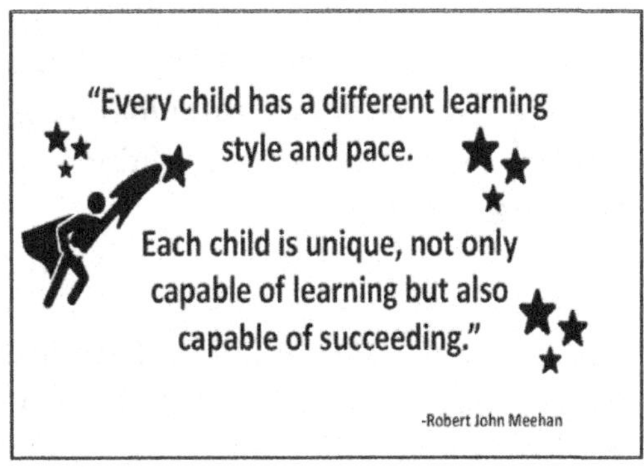

Gifted and talented students

In contrast to students with special needs, students considered gifted or talented have limited protections under state and federal laws. Federal law acknowledges that children with gifts and talents have unique needs not traditionally offered in traditional school settings. Still, there are no specific mandates or requirements for serving these children under federal law. Federal law leaves the responsibility of gifted education services to each state. Parents with gifted and talented children often feel their child's needs are not being met.

Tips for working with parents with children with special needs:

- establish clear communication. Be cautious with jargon and explain acronyms and terms to parents.
- be familiar with the child and their needs
- know the contents of their IEP or 504 Plan
- have a support system to work with the family
- respect the special education process
- provide resources and access to information to help the parent
- consult with experts or support staff for guidance
- do not try to prescribe non-educational strategies for behavior, medical, or physical problems - stay with methods that are academic and offer resources for non-academic interventions
- do not generalize different needs and be cautious with labels
- emphasize the positives of children
- understand that the frustrations families are dealing with may cause conflict and are not necessarily because of the school or staff but because of the disability

Source

U. S. Department of Education (ed.gov). Retrieved from https://sites.ed.gov/idea/statutechapter-33/subchapter-ii/1415

Home and family barriers

Working with non-English-speaking families

Schools in America are culturally and linguistically diverse. Most students become proficient in speaking English at school but talk in their native language at home. Often there is a language barrier with school staff being able to communicate with families of students from non-English-speaking homes. Similarly, non-English-speaking families feel they cannot communicate effectively with school staff when English is not their native language. Some non-English-speaking families experience low confidence because they struggle with their accents, vocabulary, and speaking fluently.

Tips for effectively communicating with non-English-speaking families:

- Be careful not to assume or stereotype different cultures.
- Know where families' languages originate (i.e., Hispanics, Mexican Hispanic, Latin Hispanics).
- For school-level material, sometimes the ELL Department offers services. Provide materials that go home to families in their native language, as feasible.
- If appropriate, provide information on websites and callouts in different languages.
- Use visual aids, icons, and signage when appropriate to aid with the language barrier.
- Find someone to help translate materials.
- Try using technology to translate materials but use caution and proofread because not all apps or software are reliable.
- Recruit an adult to help with translation. It may be appropriate for a student to help with a translation in some cases.
- When meeting face-to-face, be aware of body language, make eye contact, smile, and note voice tone and speed when talking.
- Avoid slang and educational jargon in verbal communication.
- Be selective with using educational vocabulary and acronyms in written communication—when appropriate, provide definitions and explanations.
- Color-code information that goes home to make it easier for families to understand.

"There are no language barriers when you are smiling."

— Allen Klein

According to US DOE, schools must communicate the same information about school services and programs given to limited English proficient parents to parents who are skilled in English. The information must be presented in a language and format they can understand. ***This includes information related to, but not limited to***

- registration and enrollment in school and school programs,
- grievance procedures and notices of nondiscrimination,
- language assistance programs,
- parent handbooks,
- report cards,
- gifted and talented programs,
- student discipline policies and procedures,
- magnet and charter schools,
- special education and related services, and meetings to discuss special education,
- requests for parent permission for student participation in school activities, and
- parent-teacher conferences.

"**Language** is the road map of a **culture**. It tells you where its people come from and where they are going."

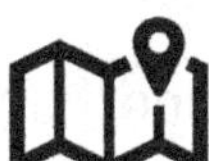

– Rita Mae Brown

Source

U.S. Department of Education (US DOE). English LEP Fact Sheet: Obligations to English learner students and limited English proficient parents. Retrieved from https://www2.ed.gov/about/offices/list/ocr/docs/dcl-factsheet-lep-parents-201501.pdf

Lack of education

The lack of education of family members could create a barrier of intimidation or low confidence in their ability to support their children's learning. Some families have members who may not have graduated from high school. Some family members might view educators as experts because they have a college degree.

"**Education** is the most powerful weapon you can use to change the world."

-Nelson Mandela

Suggestions:

- Avoid using education jargon and acronyms when communicating with families.
- Provide information to families in an easy-to-read format.
- Communicate with families in multiple ways.
- Offer GED classes for families who did not finish school.
- Offer a variety of workshops to enhance the family's capacity to learn about curriculum, standards, and assessment.
- Offer strategies and parenting tips for the families to use at home with their children.
- Consider offering literacy classes for families.

Poverty or low socioeconomic status

In 2020, the U.S. Census Bureau reported that 11.4% of Americans (1 in 8 families) live below the poverty threshold of $26,695 for a family of four. More than 14% of children, or approximately 11 million, in America live in poverty. Black and Hispanic children experience some of the highest poverty rates in the country, with 71% of the 11 million children in poverty being children of color. Poverty is classified using income thresholds based on family size and composition. If the total income of the family is below the threshold, every individual is considered poor.

Poverty can impact a child's home life, schooling, and neighborhood. The level of poverty directly influences a child's ability to learn. Similarly, education can directly affect poverty levels and the possibility of a better life. Growing up impoverished can harm a child's physical and emotional health. Typically, higher incomes are associated with better educational outcomes for children. Poverty can impede a child's ability to succeed academically and socially in a school environment.

Most parents and families desire the best possible education for their children and want academic achievement and success! What is important to remember is that this desire for most families applies regardless of their home life situation, race, ethnicity, culture, or income. Regardless of family income or background, all children need a support system to combat and reduce the impact of poverty.

Some of the challenges of children who grow up in poverty may include

- lower levels of parental involvement or attendance in school-related activities,
- entering school unprepared and are behind in skills of children not from poverty,
- experiencing feelings of isolation, alienation, insecurity, or low confidence because of their poverty,
- handling anger and frustration,
- impaired development due to stress,
- limited capacity for problem-solving and reasoning skills,
- an increased risk of dropping out of school,
- not earning a high school diploma,
- a more limited vocabulary or lower verbal skills,
- earning much lower income than people who did not grow up poor,
- health and dental problems due to poor nutrition,
- limited ability to multitask,
- scoring lower on high-stakes tests, and
- less likelihood of attending college than students from higher-income families.

> "Poverty is a very complicated issue, but feeding a child isn't."
> — Jeff Bridges, actor

Poverty causes daily hardships in the life of children and their families. These hardships create additional burdens that compound stress that can hinder the development of children growing up impoverished. In children, the consequences of compounding stress can have long-term effects on their physical and mental well-being that hinder their childhood and follow them into adulthood. Overcoming poverty is complex, and getting an education is one-way children can overcome poverty in the future. Currently, schools and communities have an opportunity and responsibility to reduce the hardships of poverty for children.

Impoverished children that are supported are more likely to

- thrive physically when their basic needs of food, clothing, and shelter are met,
- experience security when they are in a safe and nurturing environment,
- be more emotionally and socially adjusted when nurtured and loved by their parents and family, and
- flourish academically.

Educators should consider the following as it relates to poverty:

Many family structures tend to be matriarchal.

- Possibly this is due to rigid work schedules with fathers, leaving the mother to take care of the home and children.

Education is usually revered and valued but not always seen as a reality.

- Perhaps families are unaware of prospects that may be provided to their children to exceed with education. Educators can help families understand that getting an education opens the door to better life possibilities.

Believe their destiny is fate, and there is not much they can do to mitigate it.

- Imaginably many families feel their situation is permanent or do not know how to change it. Schools can help connect families with agencies and services to help their home situation.

See time in the present moment, and most decisions are based on feelings and survival.

- When families are worried about keeping a roof over their heads and food on the table, finding time to help with homework or read with their children is a lower priority.

Food is a necessity, and quantity (having enough) over quality is vital.

- For some children, their best meals are provided during school. Schools can investigate providing food pantries or weekend food packs for students. Schools can also check for food banks that families can get assistance from within their community.

Source: Payne, R. K., Devol, P., & Dreussi-Smith T. (2001). Bridges out of Poverty: Strategies for Professionals and Communities. Aha! Process, Inc.

Sources

U. S. Census Bureau (website). Retrieved 10/2021 from https://www.census.gov/data/tables/time-series/demo/income-poverty/historical-poverty-thresholds.html

Children's Defense Fund (website). Retrieved 10/2021 from https://www.childrensdefense.org/state-of-americas-children/soac-2021-child-poverty/

Poverty

Inflation, unemployment, and poverty cause many families to rely on government support or assistance from external agencies and services. Schools and staff must find ways to provide additional help to families and help them connect with support systems to ensure their student's welfare. For many children, the opportunity to get an education is the key to breaking the cycle of poverty and increasing the possibilities for helping them lead productive lives.

McKinney-Vento Homeless Assistance Act

The McKinney-Vento Homeless Assistance Act defines educational rights and provisions for children and youth experiencing homelessness. These children are guaranteed a full and equal opportunity to succeed through immediate access to a free, appropriate public education. Under McKinney-Vento, school districts must appoint a local liaison to ensure that children identified and eligible are enrolled in school, receive educational services for which they qualify, and receive referrals to health care services, dental services, mental health, and other appropriate services.

The U.S. Department of Housing and Urban Development (HUD) reported in 2020 that approximately 580,466 people experienced homelessness, about 20% were children, and 171,575 were families with children.

Here are some examples of ways schools can help families who lack resources.

- keep a food pantry on campus or send home weekend food packs.
- supply clothes or have a uniform closet; recycle uniforms or ask for donations to purchase new uniforms.
- start a prom dress consignment for students who cannot afford a dress for prom.
- give away books for families to have in the home.
- have computers on campus for families to use.
- get volunteers to help with tutoring or after-school homework help.
- make connections or provide networking opportunities with community services and agencies.
- enlist health agencies to offer free vision, dental, or other health care services.
- ask businesses to give internet to families for free or at a discounted rate.
- furnish school supplies donated (backpacks, uniforms, supplies)
- connect with agencies that offer subsidized health insurance, housing, or other assistance.
- arrange for GED courses to help families learn to speak English or become financially literate.
- make available public library cards or access to a bookmobile.
- post job opportunities and bring in speakers to help families learn how to interview or write a resume.

Sources

Office of Policy Development and Research (2021). 2020 Annual Homeless Assessment Report, Part 1 to Congress. Retrieved from https://www.huduser.gov/portal/datasets/ahar/2020-ahar-part-1-pit-estimates-of-homelessness-in-the-us.html

U.S. Department of Housing and Urban Development (2021). HUD Releases 2020 Annual Homeless Assessment Report Part 1: Homelessness Increasing Even Before COVID-19 Pandemic. Retrieved from https://www.hud.gov/press/press_releases_media_advisories/hud_no_21_041

NCHE National Center for Homeless Education (website). Retrieved from https://nche.ed.gov/mckinney-vento-definition/

Diversity

Diversity is about valuing and respecting differences. Diversity means differences in people from different social and ethnic backgrounds, cultures, genders, sexual orientations, backgrounds, and experiences. Today's schools encompass a wide range of students and families from different cultures. Staff must embrace differences and diversity among students and their families. Embracing differences offers educators a bridge to building relationships and learning about students and their families as individuals.

All parents hold strong opinions about their children's education and want them to succeed. In some cultures, educating the child is not always perceived as a shared responsibility, and collaboration or partnering with the school is viewed solely as the school's responsibility. Educators must recognize and acknowledge different cultural norms and the level of family involvement.

D = different
I = individuals
V = valuing
E = each other
R = regardless of
S = skin
I = intellect
T = talents or
Y = years

Author Unknown

Educators should be careful not to assume that families who are not visible are not interested. Instead, consider that some families may hold different beliefs about their role and the school's role in their children's education. Differences in thoughts and perceptions of responsibility may result in lower levels of parent involvement, especially for families from different cultures, low-income communities, and racial and ethnic minorities. Equally important, educators should be cautious not to stereotype families by race, ethnicity, or culture because cultural norms can vary individually with members of a subgroup and with members across and between cultural groups.

Source: *Henderson, A. T., Mapp, K. L., Johnson, V. R., & Davies, D. (2007). Beyond the Bakesale: The Essential Guide for Family-School Partnerships. The New Press, New York, NY.*

Below are some examples of diversity

in schools

- gender
- race
- intellect
- talent, skills, abilities
- disabilities
- culture
- ethnicity
- socioeconomic status
- sexual preference

in classrooms

- home life
- backgrounds
- cognitive aptitude
- level of motivation
- opinions

Schools and staff are responsible for providing a safe learning environment while promoting positive relationships among students and their families.

This involves finding ways to embrace diversity, affirm cultural differences, and address or reduce racial bias and tension so that no child or family feels vulnerable, insecure, or unsafe in the classroom or at school.

Title IX

Title IX is part of a federal civil rights law in the United States of America passed as part of the Education Amendments of 1972. Title IX is enforced through the U.S. Department of Education's Office for Civil Rights (OCR). Title IX protects people from discrimination based on sex in education programs or activities that receive federal financial assistance.

Title IX, per **https://www2.ed.gov/about/offices/list/ocr/index.html**, "No person in the United States shall, on the basis of sex, be excluded from participation in, be denied the benefits of, or be subjected to discrimination under any education program or activity receiving Federal financial assistance."

Underrepresented family groups

According to a study by the National Center for Family and Community Connections (NCFCC), most families, regardless of race, ethnicity, culture, or income, are involved in their children's schooling and wish for their children to achieve and succeed. For underrepresented and minority families, educators must work hard to engage them in more culturally relevant ways.

Below are examples of underrepresented groups of students.

- ***Minority students*** are defined as a subgroup of students whose race or ethnicity is a non-dominant race. Typically, minority groups are inclusive of:
    - Hispanic/Latinos
    - African Americans
    - Asians
    - Native Americans
    - Hawaiian/Pacific Islanders
    - those of two or more races

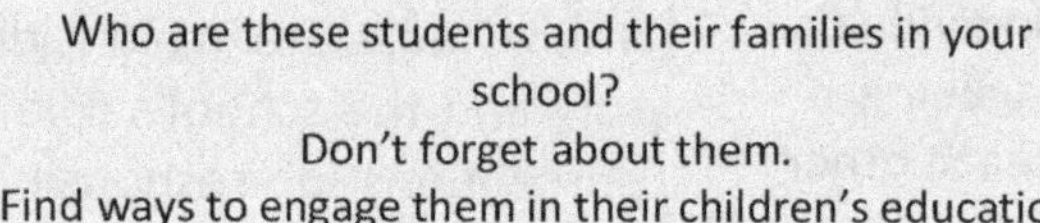

Who are these students and their families in your school?
Don't forget about them.
Find ways to engage them in their children's education.

- ***Immigrant students*** are foreign-born, whose parents are foreign-born (first generation) or born in the United States but whose parents are foreign-born (second-generation).
- ***An undocumented student*** is in the United States without legal documentation.
- ***A refugee student*** is a child in the U.S. because his family was forced to flee because of persecution, war, or violence in their country.
- ***A migrant student*** is a child who moves from one school district or area to another during the regular school year because the parent or guardian is a migratory agricultural worker or a fisher.

Underrepresented family groups, such as immigrants, Latino families, African Americans, and other minority groups, are more likely to lack knowledge of the public school system. The extent of involvement of the family and the level of outreach needed are more prominent in schools with larger minority populations. There are differences between home culture and the norms and expectations set by the school. These differences can cause misunderstandings between staff and families and sometimes wrong assumptions.

In 2021, the U.S. became overwhelmed with immigrants and undocumented minors. This influx carries over to public schools, especially in the states of Texas, Florida, California, and New York. Because the number of people coming to the U.S. is high, other states will also feel the impact. Coming from all over the world, these children are racially and ethnically diverse and are part of the millions of people coming to the U.S. each year. The school districts are tasked with providing an education for school-age children coming into their school with many needs. In addition to being non-English speaking, homeless, and impoverished, many of these children have experienced trauma.

Families are under extreme stress facing many challenges for survival outside of school, along with the language and cultural differences of living in a new country, creating overwhelming barriers to parental involvement or family engagement in their children's education. A family's home and personal challenges can cause mental and emotional distress, not just for the family or the child in school. It may also cause low confidence or distrust in the school and staff. Schools may want a parent-involvement liaison to work specifically with these families. Educators must recognize the needs of these students and their families and look for ways to help meet their needs while striving to build a vital home-school partnership that will lead a path to student success. Schools can help by reaching out to community organizations for help in meeting the basic needs of these families. Provide opportunities to connect families with resources in the neighborhood and community.

Suggestions for staff:

- Become familiar with relevant immigration policies.
- Understand immigrant students' rights.
- Learn how stress, anxiety, and trauma impact students of all ages.

Author note

Policy and immigration laws are changing. Educators should stay current on federal law and state guidelines and procedures to better serve these students and families.

Source

National Education Association. (2008). NEA policy brief 11: Parent, family, community involvement in education (Policy Brief #11 P.B. 11). National Education Association, NEA (P.B. 11). https://www.nea.org/assets/docs/PB11_ParentInvolvement08.pdf

Per the Supreme Court decision by *Plyer vs. Doe*, public schools, by law, must serve all children, including undocumented students, to avoid violation of their civil rights. As a result, specific procedures must be followed when registering immigrant children in schools.

Public schools may not:

- deny admission to a student during initial enrollment or at any other time based on undocumented status,
- treat a student differently to determine residency,
- require students or parents to disclose or document their immigration status,
- make inquiries of students or parents intended to expose their undocumented status, nor
- require Social Security numbers from all students, which may disclose undocumented status.

Source

U.S. Department of Education. Fact Sheet: FAQs about immigrant and unaccompanied youth. www2.ed.gov/policy/rights/guid/unaccompanied-children.pdf

Attitudes, feelings, beliefs, and perceptions

Families' and staff's mindsets, beliefs, perceptions, or attitudes can cause cultural and personal challenges that can be difficult to identify and address. Examining differences in opinions is essential to building relationships and forming partnerships. Staff beliefs can hinder them from productively engaging with families, and family beliefs can impair their level of involvement and engagement. A common misperception about families who are not physically present or visibly involved is that these parents do not care about their children's education. Many educators conclude that these families are not interested or do not place a high value on education. Rather than jump to conclusions, educators should carefully examine the specific causes of poor school-family relationships and low involvement levels rather than assuming families are unwilling to become more active partners with schools.

Educators must have the mindset that

- family-school partnerships are a vital practice when they support student academic achievement and success,
- education is a shared responsibility of the home, school, and community,
- all families want the best for their children and want them to succeed,
- families can support the school's efforts to increase student achievement, and
- can have a significant role in extending their children's learning beyond the classroom.

Different beliefs, perceptions, and attitudes can challenge engagement efforts !

The families must be of the mindset that

- they can and do make a difference in their children's education, and
- the school and staff value and respect them and want their support to help provide the best education for their children.

"Believe you can and you are halfway there."

-Theodore Roosevelt

Sources

Whitaker, M. & Hoover-Dempsey, K. (2013). School influences parents' role beliefs. The Elementary School Journal, 1, pp. 73-99.

Henderson, A. T. & Mapp, K. L. (2002). A new wave of evidence: The impact of school, family, and community connections on student achievement. [2002 Annual Synthesis]. National Center for Family and Community Connections with Schools. https://www.sedl.org/connections/resources/evidence.pdf

Brewster C., & Railbacks J. (2003). Building Trusting Relationships for School Improvement: Implications for Principals and Teachers. ERIC Number: ED481987

Lack of trust or confidence

Trust and confidence are essential for successful family engagement efforts and parent-teacher relationships. Trust and confidence are associated with a student's learning and behavior. A lack of trust or low self-confidence brings challenges to the partnership.

Trust

Many families lack trust or have negative feelings about school due to personal experiences. Some families do not trust the school or staff because of a negative experience with a school or educator. Similarly, some uninvolved parents and families do not come to the school because they distrust school politics or disagree with policies or educational bureaucracy. Trust is a fundamental part of any type of relationship. Trust takes time and does not come naturally. Trust is intentionally earned and preserved through actions and interactions. Students and their families must know that the school and staff care about them. In a relationship, a family-school partnership, learning to trust is a process that happens gradually through experiences and interactions with others.

Trust is challenged by	***Trust is developed by***
▪ inconsistency of policies and procedures ▪ negative past experiences ▪ words not backed by actions. ▪ poor communication ▪ discrimination ▪ unspoken expectations ▪ antagonistic interactions between staff or between staff and students and families	▪ consistency and fairness ▪ how families are treated ▪ effective communication ▪ positive first impressions of the school and meeting staff ▪ transparency ▪ active listening ▪ safe learning environment ▪ clear expectations ▪ opportunities to engage in a non-threatening environment. ▪ opportunities to observe positive interactions between staff and students, or between staff and families

Source

Gary, W., & Witherspoon, R. (2011). The power of family school-community partnerships: A training resource manual. (pp. 1–276) [NEA Priority Schools Campaign]. National Education Association—Priority School Report. http://www2.nea.org/mediafiles/pdf/FSCP_Manual_2012.pdf

Confidence

Another substantial hurdle schools face is parents' lack of confidence. Some parents and families believe that the school staff are educated professionals and may feel intimidated or lack confidence in their education or abilities. Low confidence can lead to low self-esteem. Low confidence is a mindset and the belief of being unable to do something well. Low self-esteem is when those feelings become personal and are about a person's value or self-worth. For the most part, confidence is a skill that can be developed and practiced and generally begins with having a positive or growth mindset. Like trust, building confidence happens gradually.

Confidence is challenged by	***Confidence is built by***
• negative past experiences	• identifying what you need and want.
• not knowing what you want or need.	• positive thoughts and affirmations
• being critical	• building on strengths
• focusing on negative thoughts or weakness	• considering weaknesses as opportunities to grow
• having an "I CAN"T" attitude.	• having an "I CAN" attitude or a growth mindset.
• resisting change	• embracing change
• having a defective attitude	• saying "YES" , having the willingness to try and know that failure is part of learning.
• not letting go of past failures or mistakes.	• taking risks
• comparing yourself to others	• finding a passion
• saying "NO" without trying	• being grateful, thankful, and appreciative
• not being willing to take risks.	• celebrating small successes
• not appreciating what you have	• setting goals that can be accomplished.
• having no goals	• being resilient
• feeling defeated	• developing a set of skills and strategies and practicing those skills.
• not seeking help	
• a lack of skills, strategies, or resources	

Below are some suggestions to help build trust and confidence between families and the staff.

- Know about the students and their families homelife. What do they want and need?
- Welcome families and spend time building relationships with families. Encourage partnerships with the school staff by providing opportunities for staff and families to interact.
- Listen to families' concerns and offer ways to share their concerns, give suggestions, and ask questions.
- Communicate a clear and shared mission/vision for family engagement.
- Share expectations clearly and communicate them often.
- Embrace different cultures and value differences.
- Remain professional, address issues as they arise, and demonstrate fairness and consistency.
- Build families' capacity by providing them with the skills, knowledge, and resources to enhance their abilities to be engaged in their children's learning.
- Build staff's capacity by providing them with the skills, knowledge, and resources to work more effectively in partnership with students and their families.

Challenges with school and staff

The challenges to engaging families can stem from the makeup of the school demographics, student population, families' perceptions, and staff's beliefs about engaging families.

Challenges due to school demographics such as

- the school location, surrounding neighborhoods, community resources, safety issues,
- the families' poverty level, education level, the language spoken in the home,
- and
- the student population. For example, more significant percentages in the makeup of subgroups by SWD, race, F/RL, ELL, immigrant, refugee, undocumented minors, and migrant.

Most educators want the support of families and consider parent and family engagement a vital part of their job. However, challenges to engagement arise from the lack of staff support or individual staff barriers.

Challenges with school staff supporting the engagement of families may stem when

- there is no clear school mission/vision for family-school partnership,
- leadership does not endorse or support efforts,
- there are few opportunities to engage with families,
- politics is involved, or
- there is a lack of funding, resources, or support available.

Personal barriers with staff may be due to

- their lack of capacity or skills to effectively engage with families,
- a deficit attitude or mindset,
- family engagement is considered of low importance,
- not wanting to extend efforts of outreach because it requires their time outside of school/contract hours, or
- differences in agendas or goals.

Lack of capacity—

Per Mapp and Kuttner (2013), "One of the biggest challenges with staff is their level of capacity to form effective family-school partnerships. For the most part, many educators have not been exposed to strong examples of family engagement efforts or received even minimal training in building their capacity to work effectively with families." Per Epstein (2018), another reason educators have low capacity is that "in most schools, across countries, pre-service and in-service education on family engagement is an afterthought or on the sidelines."

Beliefs—

Evaluating staff's ideas about what they consider the role of parents and families in education might uncover differences in the level of importance. A difference in beliefs is a valid reason for having a shared mission/vision for family-school partnerships that all stakeholders communicate and endorse. Developing a Partnership Plan with all stakeholders is another way of ensuring partnerships are effective and sustainable.

Level of outreach—

Educators must realize that the extent of involvement on the part of the family may depend on the school's outreach. When families are asked to be involved and understand or know what to do, it can positively affect their involvement level, extent, and quality.

Different agendas—

Some schools or teachers have their own goals or agenda for family engagement. Differing agendas can create conflict between the family and the school or teacher. For example, for some schools, the expectation is for parents to make sure their child gets to school prepared. It is expected that the roles of parents may be to support homework, attend school events and parent-teacher meetings, help the school raise money, or have fundraisers. While all these expectations and levels of involvement are reasonable, they are not getting the family engaged in their child's education in ways that support academic achievement. On the other hand, parents' goals focus on helping them ensure their child is getting a high-quality education. Some parents believe that their part is ensuring their child gets to school, and it is the job of the school and teachers to educate their child during school hours.

Here are some suggestions for addressing barriers with staff.

- Communicate the school's mission and vision for engaging families.
- Value and respect the contributions of families.
- Build staff capacity to work in partnership with families.
- Assess beliefs and perceptions in a safe environment where discussions can take place.
- Address issues as they arise.
- Ensure everyone is treated equally by honoring differences and demonstrating fairness in how everyone is treated.

Sources

Mapp, K. L. & Kuttner, P. (2013). Partners in education: A dual capacity-building framework for family-school partnerships: Version 1. SEDL.

Epstein, J. L. (2018). School, family, and community partnerships in teachers' professional work. Journal of Education for Teaching, 44(3), 397–406. https://doi.org/10.1080/02607476.2018.1465669

Find ways to address barriers

The chart below provides a list of common barriers and suggestions to address or overcome each.

Barrier	Description and suggestions
Time or busy schedules	One of the main challenges to involvement or attending school events is time and demanding schedules for families. Suggestion ▪ Offer flexible scheduling (dates, times) and more than one time.
Transportation	Not all families have multiple means of transportation. When a school is not a neighborhood school, transportation may be why families are unable to come to events. Suggestions ▪ Connect families to carpool. ▪ Use school buses to pick up families in the neighborhoods. ▪ Offer city bus passes if a school is within the city limits. ▪ Pay the expense of a taxi or Uber or possibly reimburse a family for the expense. ▪ Host activities in the neighborhood or community.
Childcare Needs	Often a barrier to getting families to come on campus or attend events is the need to care for younger siblings at home. Suggestions ▪ Offer children's activities. ▪ Provide a space for families with young children. ▪ Offer childcare on campus during an event or activity.
Language	For many families, English may not be their native language. Suggestions ▪ Offer translation. ▪ Offer workshops in other languages. ▪ Enlist the support of the ESOL or ELL Department. ▪ Provide information in the family's native language (as feasible). ▪ Consider offering family workshops to learn the English Language.

No Technology	Many families may not have access to the internet or wi-fi. <u>Suggestions</u> ▪ Offer a computer on campus for families to use. ▪ Offer workshops on computer software, using technology to monitor their child's progress, internet safety, cyberbullying, and internet etiquette. ▪ Work with businesses to offer internet access to families for free or at a discounted rate.
Lack of Communication or Information	Many parents and families do not receive information from the school or their children. Some information is not received promptly to allow them time to rearrange their schedules. <u>Suggestions</u> ▪ Provide information using multiple modes. ▪ Keep the school website updated with information. ▪ Provide families with a calendar of important dates and send reminders as the dates approach. ▪ Use technology to communicate. ▪ Advertise and market—signage, flyers, callouts, texts, and newsletters.
Disabilities	Some families have members with physical disabilities that prevent the families from engaging in or attending school events. <u>Suggestions</u> ▪ Enlist the support of the Exceptional Education Department. ▪ Know ADA requirements and check ADA compliance. ▪ Allow for accommodations and modifications for families. ▪ Offer translation or interpreters for families. ▪ Offer handicap parking and seating at events.

"The best method of overcoming obstacles is the team method."

~Colin Powell

Chapter 5

Element #3
Building Competency and Capacity

Essential Element #3 is to build the competency and capacity of staff and families.

Definition

The meaning of building competency or capacity is to improve or strengthen an organization's knowledge or the individuals within an organization and their ability to fulfill the mission and vision.

The mission and vision

The mission and vision of parent and family engagement are creating family-school partnerships, where the school staff, the students, the families, and the community, share in the responsibility of school improvement, student achievement, and academic success!

Therefore,

building families' capacity means enhancing their ability to work more effectively with the school staff to support their children's student achievement and academic success

building staff capacity means increasing their abilities and skills to form more sustainable partnerships with families and to help families support their children's learning and educational goals.

Both staff and families are made up of unique individuals, and everyone's capacity level may differ. When considering how and what to do to build the capacity of staff and families, keep in mind that staff and families are adults, and adult learning differs from children's learning. Adult learners bring life experiences to the table that impact their learning positively and negatively. It is important to remember that adults must be motivated to learn, and learning must be relevant, practical, and applicable to real life. Second, most adults are goal-oriented and want to achieve their goals. More importantly, when planning capacity-building activities, stay focused on enhancing staff and families' knowledge, skills, and resources to support student achievement and success.

Building the capacity of staff

What does staff need to work more effectively with families to support their children's education?

The purpose of building staff's capacity is so they can

- enlist the support of the family to provide the best possible education for their child,
- communicate and conference more effectively with families, and
- help families support their child's academic achievement, extend learning beyond the classroom, and set educational goals for the student.

Examples of what staff needs might include

- self-reflection on preconceived beliefs and misconceptions,
- embrace and appreciate diversity,
- creation of an environment that is safe and conducive to learning,
- understanding of cultural bias and differences,
- knowledge on the benefits of engaged families,
- ideas for engaging with families,
- training on how to share data with families,
- exposure to research-based family engagement models.,
- strategies to improve communication with families,
- family's attendance at school events and activities,
- how to host influential parent-teacher conferences,
- ways to help families support learning at home and help with homework,
- ways to help families monitor student progress like parent portals, agendas, or progress reports,
- support with behavior issues,
- ensuring that students are in attendance and to school on time, and/or
- support in ensuring students come to school well-rested, dressed appropriately, and well-groomed.

> **"Learning is not attained by chance, it must be sought for with ardor and attended to with diligence."**
>
> 
>
> - Abigail Adams

Planning staff capacity-building activities

Each staff is unique, and so are their needs and level of capacity to partner with families. Plan staff activities that align with school improvement goals and meet staff's needs.

Follow these steps for planning capacity-building activities for staff.	
Plan	**Think about?** ▪ **Purpose**—what are the staffs' needs? ▪ **Audience**—who needs it? ▪ **Format or Delivery** How will they get it? When will it happen?
Purpose	**1. What does staff need ?** For example, strategies for ☐ communicating and conferencing with families, ☐ helping families support their children's academic achievement, ☐ helping families set educational goals or extend learning beyond the classroom. **2. Consider staff barriers that might hinder efforts.**
Audience	**3. Who needs it?** ☐ whole staff ☐ a select group ☐ an individual ☐ grade level or by department
Format Delivery	**4. How will it be delivered?** **5. When or where will it happen (setting)?**
Follow-up	**6. How are activities evaluated for effectiveness?**
Resource: *Template 4B*	

The chart below shows examples of real-life staff capacity-building activities from Atwell's (2021) research.

<table>
<tr><th>Topic</th><th colspan="2">Format or delivery</th></tr>
<tr>
<td>Topics of staff training
▪ communication and conferencing
▪ cultural diversity
▪ ELL strategies
▪ student achievement/student engagement
▪ data chats
▪ relationship building and partnerships
▪ teambuilding or cooperative learning</td>
<td>School level
▪ PD by staff or principal
▪ book study

District provided
▪ Title I PowerPoint presentations
▪ district personnel or guest speaker
▪ guest speakers/trainers
▪ consultants</td>
<td>Delivery method
▪ PowerPoint presentations
▪ guest speakers
▪ training or workshop
▪ professional development
▪ faculty meeting
▪ grade level meetings
▪ department meetings</td>
</tr>
<tr><td colspan="3">Specific titles/topics
▪ Poverty Simulation (professional development)
▪ Help for Billy (book study)
▪ Kagan Cooperative Learning
▪ Accountable Talk
▪ House of Colors (team building program)
</td></tr>
</table>

Keep in mind that staff may need to enhance their skills in the same areas or topics as families. For staff to help families on a particular topic or subject they must have the capacity to do so.

"Tell me and I will **listen**.
Teach me and I will **remember**.
Involve me and I will **learn**."

-Benjamin Franklin

Building the capacity of families

The purpose of building families' capacity	
For schools	The school's goal should be to enhance families' capacity to work more effectively in partnership with school staff to support student achievement and academic success.
For classroom teachers	A teacher's goal should be to build relationships with students and their families to work as partners to support children's academic achievement and school success.
How ?	**Begin by** ▪ assessing the needs of the families, and ▪ aligning families' needs with the mission and vision for parent and family engagement. **Then,** ▪ offer activities or training, or provide skills, strategies, and resources to meet their needs.

What does building capacity mean?

Building the capacity of families means enhancing families' ability to work more effectively in partnership with the school staff to support student achievement and academic success by providing them with activities, training, skills, strategies, or resources. Partnerships begin by engaging families in activities that collaborate with the staff. Collaboration helps build trusting relationships with families, leading to forming alliances.

Why build families' capacity?

Partnership endeavors must bridge family engagement initiatives with student learning and development. Partnerships rely on both the staff and family to have the capacity to work together to reach their intended goal. Building the capacity of families requires moving efforts beyond getting families into the school to attend events to engaging them in activities that offer the sharing of knowledge, resources, and strategies to develop families' skills and enable them to support their child's academic achievement. When schools aid families and help build their capacity to support their child's academic achievement, they partner with families and engage them in the learning process, allowing them to take an active role.

Capitalizing on time and resources for families to build their capacity is an investment that pays great dividends for schools and staff as they tap into another valuable resource to aid their student achievement efforts. Students benefit when families can participate in their learning at home and school. When parents know what takes place at school, they can engage with their child's education, talk to their children about school, ask questions about their learning, and monitor assignments. This type of engagement helps extend their knowledge beyond the classroom.

The goal of capacity-building activities for families should be to help them

- support their children's academic achievement,
- assist in setting educational goals for their children,
- communicate or conference more effectively with staff,
- extend their children's learning beyond the classroom, and
- be an advocate for their children's education.

Start by identifying what families need.

Knowing what parents and families need to help their children succeed academically is the first step. By paying attention to what families need to best support their children's education, schools can provide activities supporting children's academics and cognitive, emotional, physical, or social development. Part of the capacity building of families' skills is helping families construct their role in their children's learning to include functions, such as supporters, encouragers, monitors, advocates, decision-makers, and collaborators (Mapp & Kuttner, 2013).

Most parents want to know about

- **(Expectations)** - what is expected of their child, and how to support their child's learning beyond the classroom.
- **(Monitor progress**) - how to monitor their child's progress and grades.
- **(Resources) -** where to get help or resources.
- **(Communication)** - how to communicate with the teacher and school staff, especially with questions or concerns.

Now decide what type of activity will meet the family's needs.

Keep in mind that while some families have similar needs, each family's needs are unique, as are their levels of capacity to support their children. Some capacity-building activities may be offered to entire groups, while other opportunities are offered to smaller groups or target audiences.

For example, capacity-building can occur through events and activities that are

- academic or non-academic/informational,
- advocacy allowing families to be a part of decision-making and have a voice in their children's education, and
- welcoming, to build relationships with families.

Keep in mind that enhancing families' capacity can also occur by providing support through communication, parent/family conferences, and progress monitoring.

Why offer welcoming activities?

It may seem strange that "welcoming activities" fall under the building capacity of families, considering the goal is to support academic achievement. However, through principal interviews, principals felt very strongly that welcoming activities are a large piece of the puzzle. Until families feel comfortable coming to the school for these types of activities, they will not attend academic or informational meetings. Welcoming activities allow families to engage with staff and develop relationships fundamental to forming a partnership while being involved in their children's education.

Examples of welcoming or invitational activities:

- awards ceremonies
- banquets
- festivals
- parades
- guest speakers
- student performances
- open library nights
- fine arts showcase
- sporting events
- concerts or musicals

Offer families opportunities to build their capacity!

Academic and informational activities

Academic and informational activities build families' capacity to support their children's learning and set educational goals beyond the classroom.

Examples of academic and non-academic, or informational, activities.	
Academic	**Non-academic or Informational**
Curriculum-related content area ▪ specific subjects (math, reading/language arts, science, etc.) ▪ state standards ▪ state assessments ▪ end of course exams (EOCs) ▪ test-taking skills ▪ conferencing **Parent-specific workshops** ▪ Muffins with Moms ▪ Donuts with Dads ▪ Pastries or Popcorn with Parents ▪ Granola with Grandparents ▪ Coffee with the Principal ▪ All Pro Dads	**Transition activities for** ▪ incoming kindergarten ▪ elementary to middle school ▪ middle school to high school ▪ college and career **Informational workshops** ▪ bullying, safety ▪ stress, emotional, behavior ▪ self-esteem ▪ parenting ▪ college scholarships ▪ graduation requirements **Technology** ▪ using apps ▪ social media and internet etiquette ▪ cyberbullying ▪ online learning

Other supports for families

Keep in mind that not all adult learners learn in the same way, so vary the ways support is provided to families. Some learners learn best in whole group situations. Other adults may prefer smaller or more intimate settings. Some learners require more guidance and learn best through participation and hands-on learning, while others prefer to be given the information in a quick and accessible format.

Remember that not all capacity building has to be an event or activity that requires families to come on campus or participate face-to-face. Schools should offer other ways for families to participate, like virtually or online. Another consideration is that schools can also help build families' capacity by providing other support like offering parenting tips and strategies or making resources available through the website or newsletter.

Examples of other supports to consider in helping build families' capacity.		
Home-school communication	**Progress monitoring**	**Advocacy**
Information from the school ▪ newsletters ▪ signage (on-campus, marquee, at car line) ▪ website ▪ social media ▪ APPs (example: Class Dojo) ▪ student agendas or planners ▪ callout systems	**Suggestions for monitoring progress** ▪ parent portal ▪ interim reports ▪ report cards ▪ conferences ▪ student agendas ▪ data reports	**Committees** ▪ PTA/PTO/PTSO ▪ School Advisory Council (SAC) ▪ booster clubs ▪ volunteering or mentoring **Other ways to give families a voice** ▪ surveys ▪ questionnaires ▪ suggestion box ▪ comment cards

Provide parents with suggestions for extending learning at home
▪ check student agendas or planners daily ▪ attend school events ▪ attend conferences and ask questions ▪ read at home with children ▪ ask children questions about their school day ▪ monitor the parent portal or learning management system ▪ stay in touch with children's teacher(s)

Consider including the following information on Websites
▪ provide parenting tips and suggestions ▪ include links to resources for families ▪ calendars of events ▪ important dates ▪ school contact information (hours, staff photos and emails, and phone numbers) ▪ parent and family engagement plan and compact (required if a Title I school) ▪ school handbook, policies, and procedures ▪ volunteer information

Remember

Knowing what parents and families need is crucial to providing the best support to help them help their children. Most families want to learn anything to ensure their children are getting a well-rounded education and that their needs are being met mentally, socially, emotionally, and academically. Keeping this in mind when planning capacity-building activities and providing opportunities, strategies, resources, or other support to families. On the following two pages is information included in my parent book. Look at some of the topics and sub-topics mentioned and consider if there is a need to build capacity with your students, their families, or staff.

A well-rounded education

The Every Student Succeeds Act, ESSA under Title IV, Part A calls for a well-rounded education. A well round education provides children with an enriched curriculum and diverse learning experiences that prepare them to be productive members and citizens of society who can compete globally. A well-rounded education moves beyond learning that is measured solely on test scores and core academic subjects by including the arts and music. A well-rounded education seeks to connect student learning with their curriculum, their curiosity, and their passions to promote children to become critical thinkers and engaging citizens.

ESSAs Section 8002 defines a well-rounded education as *"courses, activities, and programming in subjects such as English, reading or language arts, writing, science, technology, engineering, mathematics, foreign languages, civics and government, economics, arts, history, geography, computer science, music, career and technical education, health, physical education, and any other subject, as determined by the State or local agency, to provide all students access to an enriched curriculum and educational experience."*

Source: U.S. Department of Education, https://oese.ed.gov/offices/office-of-formula-grants/school-support-and-accountability/essa-legislation-table-contents/title-viii-general-provisions/

Social-emotional learning (SEL)

After the Covid-19 pandemic, the U.S. Department of Education, as part of the American Rescue Plan's Elementary and Secondary School Emergency Relief ESSER f provided state educational agencies (SEAS) and school districts with funds to ensure student's needs for mental, social, emotional, and academically, are being met.

People with strong social-emotional learning (SEL) are better able to cope with everyday challenges. Social-emotional skills develop self-awareness, self-control, and interpersonal skills that help students perform better in school, work, and life and benefit them academically, professionally, and socially.

Source: U.S. Department of Education. https://www.ed.gov/news/press-releases/us-department-education-releases-new-resource-supporting-child-and-student-social-emotional-behavioral-and-mental-health-during-covid-19-era

Ways parents can support their children's education.

The chart below outlines the table of contents in Atwell's (2022), *The Essential Elements of Family School Partnerships: A resource for parents and families*. The chapter titles are overarching ways parents can support their children's education. The sub-topics are what information is covered within each chapter. Consider these sub-topics as ideas for building capacity activities.

Chapter #	Sub-topics	
Chapter 7 **Learn about curriculum and instruction**	• High stakes testing • Curriculum • Standards • Instruction • Assessment and evaluation • Test scores • Grades and grading	• Critical thinking • STEM or STEAM • Learning styles • Differentiation • Accommodations and modifications
Chapter 8 **Encourage a love of literacy**	• Literacy • Language acquisition • Reading aloud with children • Literary elements • Questions • Using technologoy • Financial literacy	• Components of reading – phonics, comprehensions, vocabulary, fluency • Genres • Writing and the writing process
Chapter 9 **Support children's development**	• Academic and intellectual needs • Physical needs • Social development • Emotion and spiritual development • Resilience, GRIT, growth mindset • Leadership skills • Seven Habits of Happy Kids and Teens	• Adolencse • Friendships and relationships • Bullying • Nutrition • Healthy body image • Adequate rest • Exercise • Setting boundaries • Drugs and alcohol • Praise and love
Chapter 10 **Monitor screen time**	• Internet safety • Cyberbullying • Virtual learning	• Social media • Digital citizenship
Chapter 11 **Set educational goals**	• SMART goals • Trainsition to kindergarten, middle school, and high school	• Early education skills • Middle/high school skills • Graduation requirements
Chapter 12 **College and career**	• Choosing a path • College goals	• Saving for college • Financial aid • Interviewing for a job
Chapter 13 **Quality family time**	• Family dinner ime • Game night	• Family stories • Summer activities

Ways parents can support their children's education.

Taken from Atwell, Denise D. (2022). The Essential Elements of Family-School Partnerships: A resource for parents and families.

At home, encourage families to

- read with their child
- ask questions
- encourage a love of learning
- spend quality family time with children
- eat dinner as a family
- encourage conversations
- praise and love children
- teach children responsibility
- Set healthy boundaries
- Promote healthy growth and development
- develop GRIT and a growth mindset
- talk about healthy vs. unhealthy relationships
- practice resiliency,
- develop leadership skills
- ensure children are eating healthy and getting adequate rest
- make sure children are coming to school every day and on time
- know about available resources and support
- establish routines
- set up a quiet space with supplies for children to do their homework

Encourage families to

- **Visit campus** and get to know the school staff.
- **Be involved by**
    - attending events and activities the school offers,
    - being an advocate, and participating in school committees to have a voice.
- **Communicat**e – especially with your children's teachers.
- **Attend parent-teacher conferences** and prepare a list of questions to ask at the meeting
- **Volunteer** by sharing your time and talents.
- **Learn about curriculum and instruction.** Know what children are expected to learn and be able to do.
- **Monitor academic progress** (grades, attendance, assignments)
- **Monitor screen time and teach digital citizenship** and internet safety.
- **Set educational goals** and prepare children for college and careers.

Help families learn about the school's

- website
- policies and procedures
- data, demographics, and populations
- and how information is sent home to families
- opportunities provided
- grading
- protocol for contacting or communicating with the school and staff

local school district

- demographics and population
- funding
- Performance
- superintendent and board members
- departments
- resources
- school choices

department of education for their state of residence

- educational law
- parental rights
- state assessments and if there are implications for performance

Note: If children attend a Title I school, encourage families to become familiar with the Title I parent and family engagement plan and compact.

Plan a capacity-building activity for families

Families are unique and have different needs. The school staff's job is to form partnerships between staff and families and plan activities to successfully help families support children's learning, academic achievement, and educational success.

Follow these steps:	
Planning	**Purpose—what do they need?** **Audience—who needs it?** **Format or delivery** • What will they get? • When will it happen? • What is the takeaway for families?
Identify needs	**Start by identifying the needs of the families.** ▪ know the students and the families. ▪ collect data. ▪ conduct a needs assessment. ▪ review school improvement goals
Purpose	**Does it align with the mission and vision?** **Does it align with the school improvement goals?** **The purpose should support goals and build families capacity to** ▪ communicate or conference with staff, ▪ support their children's educational goals and academic achievement, and ▪ extend their children's learning beyond the classroom.
Type of activity	▪ academic, non-academic ▪ informational ▪ advocacy
Audience	**Who needs it?** ▪ all families ▪ target or select sub-groups (i.e., grade level, SWD, etc.)
Format or delivery	**How will they get it?** ▪ whole group or small group ▪ interactive or hands-on, virtually, online
Take-away	What is the takeaway for families? Does it support reaching partnership goals?
Resource: *Template 5*	

Build capacity through progress monitoring

Data-interpretation and sharing

Most parents want to know how their child is doing in school and progressing. Because education has become data-driven, parents and families must be educated about their child's progress. Educators need to understand data to explain and share data with parents. Communicating and interpreting data is a necessary component of parent-teacher conferencing with families.

Progress monitoring can be done through

- a parent portal or learning management system (LMS) where families can log in and see students' grades or attendance,
- some type of report card and interim or mid-term reports (**not**e, typically these reports only provide parents with letter grades for subject areas but do not show growth or progress), and
- conferences.

As much as possible, grading should be

- consistent and fair (within a school, district, and across classrooms),
- measured against a set of standards (parents should be aware of these standards), and
- able to provide feedback on how a student is doing and how they can improve

The purpose of grading is to inform parents of their children's

- **academic progress** (measured against standards or individual goals),
- **academic growth** (comparison to self or in comparison to the norm of peers), and
- **academic achievement** (standardized scores, percentiles, or scaled scores).

In addition to academic grading, parents should be informed of their children's

- personal development (as measured against the norm of peers or individual goals),
- work and study habits,
- character traits and social skills, and
- behavior.

Traditionally, schools use a grading system based on letter grades:

- **"A" to "F"**
- **E (excellent)**
S (satisfactory), or
N (needs improvement)

Some examples of different types of grading of progress monitoring for classrooms

- benchmark assessing
- rubrics
- portfolios
- self-grading
- pass/fail
- anecdotal records
- formative/summative assessments
- feedback (evaluative or descriptive)

REMEMBER, that grading provides a way to monitor a child's academic achievement and success. Parents must understand how grades, or progress, are measured. When presenting parents and families with data, provide the necessary background and terms to fully understand what the data are and what the data tells.

It is not what you do for
your children,
but what you have taught
them to do for themselves,
that will make them
successful human beings.

— *Ann Landers*

Build capacity through conferences

Parent-teacher conferences are great opportunities for families to meet with a teacher or team of teachers and learn how their child is doing in school. Conferences should be a two-way conversation that allows both the family members and the teacher an opportunity to speak, listen, and be heard. The purpose of a conference is to provide families with information and strategies to help their child, share data showing how their child is performing, and allow families to ask questions and share concerns. Remember, parents and families, are a child's first teachers. They have a vested interest in their children's education and life success and can offer knowledge about their children that is not available to anyone else. Allow them to share this knowledge.

A conference is

- a planned opportunity to meet with families,
- a way to learn more about the student and gain insight from the family into the child's home life,
- designed with an emphasis on student learning and success,
- a two-way conversation gives families a chance to express their concerns and ask questions,
- centered on the student and discussing with the family the student's progress, academically and socially, and highlighting strengths and areas where improvements are needed,
- a way to provide families with strategies on how they can extend learning beyond the classroom and an opportunity to share student data about how the student is progressing academically, and
- a chance to develop a plan or goals to help the student succeed.

Begin planning a conference by answering the following questions:

1. **Purpose** - Why is a meeting necessary?
2. **Format** - What type of conference format will best accomplish the conference's goal or purpose?
3. **Takeaway** - What will families take away from the conference?

1. Purpose –

Parent/family conferences should be an efficient and interactive process that provides an educational plan or path to students' success. Conferencing with parents and families offers an opportunity for parents, teachers, and others who support a child's learning to share and learn more about how a child is doing in school and how learning can be supported at home. Conferences should not be random acts or opportunities but purposeful and planned. Sometimes setting a date and time for a formal conference is the only way to get families to come to school or get involved. Establishing protocols and procedures for communication and conferencing can focus on the student and support the student's learning, academic achievement, and success.

2. Format –

There are many different conference formats; the most common type is a face-to-face parent-teacher conference. However, other conference formats are student-led portfolios, data chats, or academic team meetings.

<table>
<tr><th colspan="2">Examples of types of conferences:</th></tr>
<tr><td>Face-to-face</td><td>Most common conference formats:<ul><li>face-to-face (in person)</li><li>face-to-face (online)</li></ul>Usually, the teacher or an administrator facilitates the meeting.<ul><li>parent-teacher</li><li>parent/family - teacher(s)</li><li>parent/family - administration</li><li>parent/family - teacher - student</li></ul>Sometimes middle/high school conferences involve a team of teachers. Consider inviting the other teachers so that the parents can meet with everyone together. Or schedule conferences with multiple teachers on the same date in succession.</td></tr>
<tr><td>Portfolio</td><td>A portfolio conference can be facilitated by the teacher or student. I n this type of conference, a student portfolio is shared with the family. The portfolio can contain work samples, data, and assessments. The student designs some portfolios to showcase his/her best work. Other portfolios contain specific student work samples to illustrate progress.</td></tr>
<tr><td>Student-led</td><td>The student facilitates the conference and shares his/her work samples or portfolio with family members who attend.</td></tr>
<tr><td>Data chats</td><td>Data chats are typically teacher-led with a family and held in small groups with several families in attendance. Each family is provided data on their child. In larger groups, class data may be presented holistically for the class and disguising data information identifying children personally. Only the parent would know which data represents their child and can see where their child is performing in relation to his peers without identifying them</td></tr>
<tr><td>, Academic teams</td><td>For an excellent example, search for Academic Parent-Teacher Teams (APTT) by Dr. Maria Paredes</td></tr>
</table>

3. Takeaway -

Families should attend a conference to understand how their child is doing academically, socially, and behaviorally. Families should also go with an understanding of their child's expectations and how they can support those expectations.

REMEMBER - Identify barriers

Consider possible barriers that will hinder efforts to maximize the conference. Identifying barriers ahead of time will help find ways to overcome those barriers.

Consider

- Offering a choice of dates, times, or locations to make it convenient for families.
- Working schedules can hinder families from attending face-to-face conferences. Consider another time or place to hold the meeting, such as a home visit, off-campus location, or virtually.
- Planning an activity or something to keep siblings or small children busy during a conference.
- Getting someone to help with translation if the parent does not speak English.
- Involving resource teachers or counselors if an academic plan will be developed.

Angry Parents

Unfortunately, sometimes a conference is scheduled due to problems that need to be addressed. In many instances, parents or family members who attend are upset and angry. As educators, we must remain positive and professional and use the conference to remedy the situation by discussing any problems or concerns.

Tips

- **ALWAYS** have something positive to say about the child and **ALWAYS** stay positive.
- Actively listen to the parents and give them a chance to share their feelings.
- Listen before proposing a solution.
- Document the child's behavior and conversations about it. Describe the problem in non-judgmental ways.
- Do not talk or write to a parent when angry.
- Talk to other teachers who have worked with or have a relationship with the child to gain insight.
- Imagine the viewpoint of the parent if the roles were reversed.
- Ask another teacher or the principal to sit in on the conference if there is any indication it might not go as planned.
- On some occasions, it may be necessary to have an administrator or support person sit in on a conference, especially if there is a problem or a hostile parent.

Effective vs. ineffective conferences

What is needed to make the conference effective?

Ineffective conferences	***Effective conferences***
(Common mistakes) • Have no purpose, agenda, or not planning. • Fall behind schedule. • Are held in an unwelcoming environment. • Teacher-centered rather than parent-student focused • Do not allow parents to ask .questions or share concerns. • The focus is only on problems and not on solutions. • Do not sharing data to support areas that the child needs improvement. • Have no goal or action plan for follow-up.	• Are planned with a purpose. • Follow an agenda that values everyone's time and input. • Make parents feel welcome a • allow parents to participate and give input. • Provide parents with information about how their child is performing, and where their child struggles and offer tips and strategies on how they can help their child.

"Family/school relationships are the foundation for real family engagement! Without relationships there is no engagement!"

-Steven Constantino

Tips for successful conferences

Try to

- give advance notice of the date/time for the conference.
- start and end the meeting on a positive note.
- decide on a conference format and prepare an agenda.
- be prepared and organized ahead of time.
- be an active listener and ask questions.
- prepare an agenda to keep the conference on track.
- keep conversation straightforward and be careful of educational jargon.
- have the classroom clean and the seating organized.
- pay attention to body language and voice tone.
- start and end on time (have a clock or timer visible)
- share data but explain it in terms understandable to the parent.
- have samples of student work to back up talking points.
- provide a takeaway such as homework tips, tools, resources, or strategies that will help families extend classroom learning after the conference.
- seek additional support if needed—ask the principal, guidance counselor, or another teacher to sit in.
- take notes and provide a way for parents to take notes.
- allow the parent to ask questions or share concerns.
- anticipate the family bringing the student or siblings with them and having something for them to do during the conference.
- share the child's strengths and unique qualities.

Try not to

- get off-topic; stick to the agenda.
- become emotional or argue.
- start late or go over time.
- overwhelm the parents with too many tasks.
- cover too much in the conference or drag it out too long.
- use educational jargon.
- make promises.
- share personal experiences.
- say anything that the child should not know.
- let parents leave empty-handed—allow them to go with information, resources, or work samples.
- be careless when sharing weaknesses or areas of concern.
- end on a negative note.

Plan a successful conference

Every successful meeting or conference should follow a set agenda with both parties coming prepared with something to say.

Before the conference

Checklist

- Notify the parents and students of the purpose, place, time, and length of the conference.
- Plan the conference—prepare an agenda or conference sheet.
- Think about what to say and how to avoid education jargon.
- Think about what points need to be discussed at the conference.
- Gather materials—data to support talking points.
- Consider sharing the agenda with the family before the conference to let them know what will be addressed and to prepare questions. Or provide a planning sheet with some questions to prepare for the meeting or to ask during the conference.

After the conference

- Immediately after the conference, thank everyone for coming.
- A few days after the conference, follow up with any questions or concerns discussed to add additional thoughts or include suggestions and resources to help the family.

Consider each of the following when planning a conference

Plan

Format

- face-to-face
- online

Location

- school—classroom, media center, office
- off-campus
- home visit

Conference dates/times

- before, during, or after school

Gather materials before the conference.

- work samples, information, or data
- give families something to take home.

Prepare a conference agenda

It is so easy to get off-topic or lose track of the focus during a conference. Planning and preparing a conference form or agenda will help keep the meeting on track by providing talking points.

Be sure to address the following as part of an agenda.

Example agenda

Open with a welcome,

- establish a protocol (time limits, format, refer to the agenda, etc.)
- if you are not providing them a copy of the conference notes, encourage notetaking.

Discuss strengths and areas of concern.

- begin on a positive note—start with strengths.
- share strengths and unique qualities of the child..
- then ease into sharing concerns.
  - expectations (behavior, participation, learning difficulties, and homework)
  - academics/grades
  - have data to back up talking points.

Develop an action plan.

- choose one or two areas to focus on
- discuss follow-up or next steps.

Allow the family to ask questions and share concerns.

Summarize talking points and next steps. Give the parents a copy of the conference form or log to take with them.

Thank the parents/family for coming.

Use a conference form or log

Have a conference form to use during the conference for notes. Offer a copy to the family to take home with them and keep a copy for your records. Some schools create their form on NCR paper with duplicate or triple copies, allowing the parents to leave with the conference notes. The internet is full of example conference agendas and forms. Use an already designed example to help create one that meets your needs.

Help families prevent the summer slide

The summer slide, or summer learning loss, refers to the loss of learning and instructional time for children during summer vacation when schools are closed. Summer learning loss is prevalent with elementary-age students, specifically younger children, especially in reading. However, a learning loss can also be attributed to lower-income students due to limited enrichment, experiences, or resources they have access to over the summer. Schools have an excellent opportunity to build families 'capacity to understand the learning loss during the summer and provide information, skills, and resources to use with their children. There are so many ways to encourage summer learning, and below are some examples of ways schools can help.

Here are some ideas and suggestions to provide families.

- a list of community resources or a calendar of events; include ideas for field trips to museums, art galleries, or summer camps; or a public library or bookmobile schedule.
- summer learning packets, summer reading books and questions, and activities with the books.
- materials to practice math skills, materials to make flashcards, or learn games.
- academic links, websites, or apps.
- STEM or science activities.
- a list of free movies and literacy activities to go along with the movies.
- summer journals, and
- academic scavenger hunts.

Remember parents to

- encourage their children to read.
- limit TV, social media, and time with electronics

Below are some examples of encouraging free and fun activities for families and their children. Example activities:

- plan menus, and grocery lists, then cook a meal.
- play board games and card games.
- take free field trips.
- keep a summer journal.
- take a virtual vacation or plan a dream vacation; create a budget and itinerary, and design postcards and travel brochures.
- write letters and seek a pen pal.
- spend time outdoors, camp in the backyard, or watch a sport and gather data, statistics, and averages, and create charts.
- use the newspaper to chart current events, weather, and stocks.
- volunteer
- visit places in your community

Section 3
Getting the Gears in Motion

Section 3 is the toolbox.

Chapter 6 - An "owner's manual" that provides an overview of the essential elements and information covered in the previous chapters.

Chapter 7 - How to collect data to develop a plan for partnership. This chapter discusses step-by-step directions on how to collect data on your school, students, and families and how to evaluate current engagement practices to develop a partnership plan.

Chapter 8 - is the example templates for school level and classroom level, the tools to aid in Steps 1-5 of creating a partnership plan.

How to get started

Before any program can be put into place, it must be well thought out and planned to be successful. Even the most well-laid-out plans must go through a tune-up to keep them running smoothly. It does not matter if the goal is to establish new partnerships with students and their families or if the goal is to strengthen existing partnerships.

Step #1 – Form a parent and family engagement team.

Step #2 – Write or revise your mission/vision for parent and family engagement.

Step #3 – Collect and review data.

Step #4 – Develop a partnership plan.

Step #5 – Share, implement, and monitor the plan for effectiveness.

Coming together is a **beginning.** Keeping together is **progress.** Working together is **success!**

-Henry Ford, American Industrialist

Chapter 6

The "Owner's Manual" – A Review

Let us review.

Who is responsible for family-school partnerships?

All stakeholders are responsible for school improvement and student achievement. However, family-school partnerships begin between the school and home. Home means the family and school means all staff.

The school leader is responsible for

- bringing together all involved stakeholders (staff, families, community, and business partners),
- initiating engagement efforts and communicating the mission and vision for family-school partnerships,
- knowing the needs of staff and families,
- building the capacity of staff and families to work in collaboration, and
- building their level of capacity to establish and sustain family-school partnerships that support student achievement and school improvement.

Teachers are responsible for building trusting relationships with their students and families and

- identifying what the students and families need and considering any challenges that affect their engagement.
- ensuring effective two-way communication.
- building families' capacity to allow them to set educational goals, extend learning beyond the classroom, monitor their children's academic progress, and
- build their level of capacity to work in partnership with families.

What do partnerships need to be effective and sustainable?

1. **A shared purpose** – This is why it is important to have a mission and vision statement for parent and family engagement that
   - aligns with school improvement goals,
   - has buy-in from all stakeholders, and
   - is communicated to all stakeholders.

2. **The purpose of the partnership should benefit all stakeholders by meeting the needs of students and families and staff and improving academic achievement and being successful in school. This is why addressing the essential elements and their components is relevant and why the elements must be in working in tandem (like gears).**

Let's review the Essential Elements. SECTION 1

The essential elements and their components were developed through research to discover what and how schools establish and sustain partnerships that met the goal of improving the school and helping ensure that children reach their potential.

The essential elements are

- to create a culture and climate that welcomes families,
- to consider challenges that hinder engagement efforts, and
- to build competency and capacity of staff and families.

Addressing the essential elements helps

- create a culture and climate that is welcoming to all families and provides opportunities to build relationships among staff and students and their families as the first step,
- meet the needs of staff, students, and families, consider the challenges that hinder engagement, and find solutions to overcome some barriers,
- staff have a greater capacity to work in partnership with families in support of academic achievement and success, and
- enhance families' ability to support their children's learning beyond the classroom, set education goals, and work in partnership with the school to provide the best possible education for their child.

Resource: Refer to the chart in Section 1.

Element #1 Check the culture and climate. CHAPTER 3

The climate and culture are the environment of the school campus and classrooms and the feeling one gets when they are in that environment and how they are treated. The environment should welcome all families, embrace diversity, and make families feel valued and respected.

Family-school partnerships are more effective when the school culture and climate has

- the support of leadership,
- a communicated mission and vision for family engagement,
- a welcoming environment that values and respects all families,
- opportunities for families to come on campus or be engaged in their children's education,
- time and effort invested in building trusting relationships with families, and
- effective (two-way) communication between the home and school.

The key is to build relationships and have effective communication.

Tips for effective communication

- remember that communication is two-way, from home to school and from school to home.
- send communication that goes home to families using multiple methods and in families' native languages as feasible.
- give parents access to staff by providing various means to communicate with staff like email, phone, text, or parent portal.
- ensure there is a way for families to ask questions or share concerns.
- utilize technology.
- have a user-friendly school website, kept updated with current information, and offer parents tips and strategies to support their children's education.

Element #2- Consider the challenges that hinder engagement efforts. CHAPTER 4

For partnerships to be effective, schools must **identify barriers** that hinder engagement efforts and meet those challenges by looking for possible solutions.

Challenges or barriers exist for the home, school, student, and family.
Examples may include:

Obstacles—perceptions, beliefs, misconceptions, or attitudes
Factors—poverty, language, educational level, race, student age, or grade level
Hurdles—transportation, work schedules, childcare, or language.

How?
Collect data for developing a partnership plan.

1. Evaluate current parent and family engagement practices to find out what is working, where improvements are needed, and how current practices address the essential elements.
2. Review school demographics and student population to help identify barriers.
3. Conduct a needs assessment with staff and families to discover what hinders their engagement efforts and what they need to work more effectively in partnership.

Most importantly, is to get to know families by

- offering meet-and-greets.
- having staff visible on campus, at the car drop-off or pick-up line.
- providing opportunities to engage with students and their families.
- talking with families, knowing them by name, and pronouncing their names correctly.
- finding out what they need and want by conducting surveys, seeking their input, collecting personal inventories from families, and
- having team-building activities at school events.

Element #3 Build the competency and capacity of staff and families to work in partnership. CHAPTER 5

The goal is to build the competency and capacity of staff and families to work in partnership to support student achievement and success.

For families

Building capacity means enhancing the knowledge and skills of families and staff to work in partnership by providing them with strategies, training, or resources to

- ✓ extend learning beyond the classroom,
- ✓ support academic achievement, and
- ✓ set educational goals for success.

For staff

Building capacity means enhancing the knowledge and skills of staff to work in partnership with families by providing them with strategies, training, or resources to

- ✓ communicate effectively with families, and
- ✓ help families support their children's educational goals, academic achievement, and success.

Build staff's capacity. CHAPTER 5

The school leader should provide opportunities to enhance their staff's capacity to work more effectively with families. Capacity-building activities should align with the mission and vision for family-school partnerships and school improvement goals.

Common examples of staff capacity-building activities are learning to

- effectively communicate with families,
- to appreciate culture and diversity,
- understand poverty and how it affects education,
- partner with non-English-speaking families, underrepresented families, and families of special needs children
- to conference with families and help them set educational goals for their children,
- help families monitor the progress of their children,
- share and explain data with families, and
- deal with difficult parents.

Build families' capacity. CHAPTER 5

Schools should provide opportunities to families. The opportunities offered should be designed to meet the student's and families' needs and aligned with the mission and vision for family-school partnerships.

Family capacity-building activities can be opportunities classified as

- **welcoming** (activities and events that allow for building relationships),
- **volunteering** (ways to engage families with staff and allows for building trust and relationships)
- **academic and non-academic** (meetings, workshops, and activities that link directly with student achievement and academic success),
- **conferences** (opportunities for families to meet with school staff, discuss their child's progress, set educational goals, and share concerns), and
- **advocacy** (ways families can have a voice or be part of decision-making).

Plan capacity-building activities based on a need

To build the competency and capacity of staff or families and know what they need to work in partnership and support student achievement.

How to know what staff or families need?
Plan activities to meet the needs of staff and families. A review of the data collected and analyzed before developing a plan Is very helpful.

Consider:

- ✓ the needs of staff and families,
- ✓ barriers and challenges,
- ✓ academic needs, and
- ✓ school improvement goals.

To plan a capacity-building activity, consider the following:

Purpose What do they need?
Audience Who needs it?
Format How will they get it?

Delivery What will they get?
When/where will it happen?

Take-away For families—what is the takeaway?
For staff—what is the follow-up?

Resources **What will it take to make it happen?**

- materials/supplies, funding, people, volunteers, helpers

An Overview of The Essential Elements of Family-School Partnerships

Effective family-school partnerships rely on the essential elements and their components working in tandem.

GOAL:
Create a culture and climate on the school campus and in classrooms that welcome all families and provides them with opportunities to build relationships and form partnerships with staff that supports their children's academic achievement and success.

The culture and climate are shaped by.

- the support of leadership,
- a communicated mission and vision for family engagement,
- everyone working towards the goal of supporting student achievement and success,
- time and effort invested in building trusting relationships with families,
- providing opportunities for families to be engaged in their children's education, and
- effective communication between the home and school, and families and staff.

GOAL:
Determine what hinders engagement efforts and what staff and families need to work more effectively in partnership to support student achievement.

How?

Collect and review data.

<u>Data should include:</u>

- An evaluation of current practices is measured against the essential elements to discover what is working and where improvements are needed.
- A review of school and student demographics and population.
- A needs assessment to determine what staff and families want and need.

Offer families opportunities to be involved by providing.

1. **Welcoming activities** (to build relationships)
2. **Volunteering** – Ways to participate in helping the school or classroom and a time for building relationships.
3. **Academic and Non-Academic** Workshops/Activities (to build capacity plan activities that meet the needs of students and their families.
4. **Advocacy** -Ways to have a voice in their children's education.

<u>Use the data to</u>

- Determine the needs of staff and families and provide opportunities to meet those needs.
- Identify barriers and find solutions to overcome barriers.
- Develop a partnership plan, that includes how to
  - Build the capacity of staff and families based on the identified needs.
  - Connect business and community resources with the needs of students and their families.

GOAL:
To build staff's capacity is to enhance their knowledge and skills to help families support their children's academic achievement by providing training, strategies, and resources to do so effectively.

To build families' capacity is to enhance their knowledge and skillset to support their children's learning beyond the classroom, set educational goals, and ensure academic achievement and success.

Schools should provide both staff and families opportunities to build their capacity to work in partnership to support students' academic achievement and success. These opportunities should be based on what staff and families need planned with a purpose -why; audience-who; format-how/when; and a takeaway -that aligns with the purpose.

Let us get started

Here are the steps to help you get started. These same steps apply regardless of if you are establishing a new partnership or revisiting your current partnership efforts and giving them a tune-up. Keep in mind that if your school is a Title I school, the Title I plan will be your partnership plan for step #4. For non-Title I schools a template for a partnership plan is provided.

Step #1 – Form a parent and family engagement team.
Step #2 – Write or revise your mission/vision for parent and family engagement.
Step #3 – Collect and review data.
Step #4 – Develop a partnership plan.
Step #5 – Share, implement, and monitor the plan for effectiveness.

Ideally, writing or revising a family-school partnership plan should be done annually as part of school improvement. The reason the plan should be revised annually is that every school year new students and families are entering your school. It is important to consider the families you will be serving when planning. A plan should be implemented and monitored for effectiveness. Meaning there will be tweaks that need to be made along the way but for the most part, a working partnership plan is in place for an academic school year.

Step #1 - consider forming a family engagement team.

A family engagement team should be comprised of school leaders, teachers, staff, and family members. The majority (51% or more should be parents and family members that are representative of your student population and subgroups). *For information about a family engagement team refer to #3 advocacy in Section 1- Chapter 1.*

It is important to allow families to network with other parents and members of the businesses and communities that support their children's education. Utilize all available resources in your community and never underestimate the value of human capital. Tap into the hidden potential of your families and other stakeholders to bring to the team. Never forget that partnerships require the buy-in and input of all stakeholders so include them in the planning process.

Resource: Template 1

Staff		Parents/Family	Community/Business
Leadership			
Teachers			
Support Staff			
Totals			

Step #2: Create or revise a vision and mission for partnerships.

The mission defines the task/purpose that describes what we do, how we do it, and for whom we do it. **The vision** communicates what we want to accomplish (a goal) and how we want to get there (objectives).

The mission and vision statement for family-school partnerships should

- align with school improvement goals,
- get buy-in from all stakeholders, and
- communicate the mission and vision to all stakeholders.

The vision and mission statement should be

- developed with all stakeholders, as everyone should have buy-in to make the mission and vision a reality,
- personalized and reflect the needs of the school, staff, and family, and
- aligned with school improvement goals.

> **"To accomplish anything, you must first have a mission, a vision, a hope, and a goal."**
>
> -Rick Warren

Resource: Template 1

Step #3- Collect and review data

After a team has been put into place and team members have reviewed the mission and vision for family-school partnerships the goal should be clear – to develop a plan to establish and sustain partnership efforts are being maximized to their fullest potential.

To improve any program is to evaluate and reflect on what works and does not, then adjust along the way. The same idea applies to keeping a family-engagement program working like a well-oiled machine. Relationships require work, and ongoing reflection is vital for improving the plan. Problems and challenges exist and require the capacity to identify problems or challenges and address those challenges by finding solutions.

The purpose of collecting data is to identify

- the needs of the children and families,
- what students need to help them succeed academically,
- what support families need from the school and staff, and
- what staff needs to form partnerships with families.

> **Data by itself is useless.**
> **Data is only useful if you apply it!**
>
> 
>
> -Todd Banks

Start here

The next step is to evaluate current practices to determine what is working and where improvements can be made. Everything in education is data-driven. While data is only one piece of a puzzle, looking at data can help schools learn more about the students and families they serve, discover the needs of these students and families, and identify barriers that hinder engagement efforts.

What data should be collected?

Collect and review the following data.

A. **the goals and objectives of the School Improvement Plan** (SIP)
B. **data on student population, demographics, assessment scores, and data trends**
C. **an assessment of current practices**—what works and does not work or needs improvement. *An evaluation is provided as templates 2A and 2.*
D. **conduct a needs assessment** to determine what students, staff, and families need to work in partnership to effectively support student achievement and success.

How do you analyze the data?

Use the following resources: Data collection sheet provided as Template 3A and 3B.

- What does the data tell you?
- Where is there a need?
- Be sure to look at the data holistically but also look at subgroups and individual families.
    - What do they need and who needs it?
    - When you identify needs you also want to find ways to meet those needs.

Note

School-level data represents sub-groups of students and parents holistically for all grades in the school.

Drill deeper and look at classroom or grade level data to target specific students and families and identify their needs individually.

Why or how does this data help develop a partnership plan?

A. School Improvement Plan

Family school partnerships are part of school improvement. The goals in a school improvement plan should incorporate the engagement of families to support student achievement and success. By the same token, family-school partnerships should also be working towards the same goals as outlined in the school improvement plan, but a partnership plan should include the roles and responsibilities families can play in improving the school and ensuring the best possible education for all children.

B. School and student data

It is important to know the students and families you serve. One way is to review student population and demographics data. See the chart below for some examples. Also, refer to Essential Element #2 Chapter 2 for more information.

Student Population	Family Demographics	Data Trends
▪ students (male, female) ▪ age/grade level ▪ race (White, African American, Hispanic, Other) ▪ ELL (English Language Learners, Level) ▪ SWD (types of disabilities) ▪ poverty level (F/RL) ▪ immigrant/migrant/refugees	▪ culture ▪ language (non-English-speaking) ▪ economics—poverty ▪ educational level ▪ work schedules ▪ talents—skills	▪ assessment data (strengths and weaknesses) ▪ attendance ▪ behavior (incident reports)

C. Evaluate current engagement practices

Assess the current practices for engaging parents and families against the essential elements and their components. Remember, the elements and their components must work in tandem to maximize effective partnerships.

Templates 2 A and 2 B have been provided to help evaluate current practices at the school level and or for the classroom, grade levels, or by department.

D. Conduct a needs assessment to determine the needs of staff and families.

Sometimes the only way to find out what staff and families need and want is to ask them. Consider offering opportunities for them to give their input using a questionnaire or survey.

The needs assessment should answer the following questions.

Staff	Families
What does staff need to enhance their capacity to partner with families? • skills and knowledge • resources • training or professional development	**What do families need to be more engaged in and enhance their capacity to support their children's learning?** • skills, strategies • knowledge, information, resources

Suggestions for gathering data

- survey staff and families,
- create small focus groups or committees,
- do some outreach for hard-to-reach families to gather input,
- for staff, hold discussion or focus groups, team meetings, and
- for families, host small group or town hall meetings, conduct surveys, use questionnaires, or use suggestion boxes.

Lastly, combine all the data collected from the *evaluation of current practices (Template 2A or 2B), school and student data (Template 3A or 3B), and the needs assessment.*

Questions: *What is currently happening to engage families in their children's education? What is working (strengths)? Where are improvements needed?*

+ strengths		- needs improvement
#1: Culture and Climate - Welcoming families and building relationships		
culture/climate		
communication		
#2: Challenges - Identifying and addressing barriers that exist		
school		
staff		
students		
families		
#3: Confidence and Capacity - Opportunities to build capacity		
for families		
for staff		

Now, use the findings of your data to develop or revise a partnership plan.

Step #4: Develop a partnership plan

The components of the plan:

1. **begin with a vision/mission statement** for family-school partnerships.

2. **address the essential elements.**
   a. targets ways to improve the culture and climate, communication, and build relationships.
   b. identified barriers and possible solutions.
   c. planned capacity-building activities for staff and families.

3. **assign roles and responsibilities to all stakeholders.**

The partnership plan should be:

- ✓ a working document that is written and revised annually.
- ✓ developed with input from all stakeholders, including administration, staff, teachers, families, and community members.
- ✓ shared with all stakeholders.
- ✓ implemented, monitored, and evaluated for effectiveness.

The purpose of a ***partnership plan*** is to maximize parent and family engagement efforts through thoughtful planning with attention to the essential elements.

A well-developed partnership plan

- communicates the mission and vision for engaging families in their children's education,
- improves the school culture and climate by encouraging building relationships between the school staff and the students and families,
- identifies barriers that hinder engagement efforts and seeks to find solutions, an
- plans opportunities to build staff and families' capacity to work as partners to support student achievement and success.

Author Note
Title I public schools should have a Title I parent and family engagement plan and a compact.

The partnership plan is most effective when it is

- a working document that is shared with all stakeholders,
- implemented with fidelity and monitored and evaluated for effectiveness,
- developed with input that includes administration, staff, families, and community members, and
- written and revised annually.

With the Family Engagement Team, it is now time to use the data to create a plan for partnership or revise an existing plan.

Resources: Templates 4A and 4B are provided as examples of a partnership plan that addresses the essential element and their components.

To plan capacity-building activities please see Templates 5A and 5B.

Remember capacity building activities should be planned to meet a need of staff and/or families and enhance their abilities to support students. When planning capacity-building activities consider the following:

a. purpose - why
b. audience- who
c. format- how
d. takeaway- does it meet the need or purpose

A goal without a plan is just a wish!

-Antoine de Saint-Exupéry

See Chapter 5 for additional details

Step #5: Share, implement, and monitor the plan

When the plan is complete, the last step is to share, implement, and monitor the plan for effectiveness by

- sharing the plan with all stakeholders and communicating the importance of the plan,
- implementing the plan and making it a living document,
- monitoring the implementation of the plan,
- frequently revisiting the plan, and
- reflect on the plan and revise it to fix what works and does not.

"Our goals can only be reached through a vehicle of a plan, in which we must fervently believe, and upon which we must vigorously act. There is no other route to success."

~ Pablo Picasso

Chapter 8

The Templates

Here are sample templates, most notably the partnership plan for schools and classrooms or grade/department levels. Except for the "Partnership Plan," the other templates aid in collecting and evaluating data needed for developing or revising the plan. As previously mentioned, much of the partnership plan design is based on Title I compliance requirements. Title I public schools should already have a school-level Parent and Family Engagement Plan (PFEP) and compact and will notice some similarities in the "Partnership Plan." Below is a description of each template.

TEMPLATE #1: Writing a mission and vision statement.
This template is designed to help the "family engagement team" write or revise a mission and vision statement for family-school partnerships.

TEMPLATE #2: Evaluation of current practices

- ✓ *2A: School level*
- ✓ *2B: Classroom, grade level, or department*

These templates are checklists to evaluate current practices using the three essential elements. The purpose is to discover what is working and where improvements are needed.

TEMPLATE #3: Data collection sheet

- ✓ *3A: School level*
- ✓ *3B: Classroom/grade level*

These templates are to collect data on school and student demographics and populations.

TEMPLATE #4: Partnership plan

- ✓ *4A: School level*
- ✓ *4B: Classroom or grade level*

These partnership plans were developed to help schools or classroom/grade levels design a plan by providing step-by-step guidance to address the three essential elements necessary for establishing and sustaining effective family-school partnerships. The plan aims to engage with their students and families more effectively by forming a family-school partnership that supports student achievement and success.

TEMPLATE #5: Planning a capacity-building activity.

- ✓ *5A: for families*
- ✓ *5B: for staff*

These templates will help plan with detail a capacity-building activity for staff or families.

Template #1 - Writing a mission and vision statement

<table>
<tr><th colspan="4">School Level
Family Engagement Team & Mission/Vision</th></tr>
<tr><td colspan="4">School

Academic School Year</td></tr>
<tr><td colspan="4">Family Engagement Team Members
(Ideally, the family and community/business membership should represent at least 51%.)</td></tr>
<tr><th colspan="2">Staff</th><th>Parents/Family</th><th>Community/Business</th></tr>
<tr><td>Leadership</td><td></td><td rowspan="3"></td><td rowspan="3"></td></tr>
<tr><td>Teachers</td><td></td></tr>
<tr><td>Support Staff</td><td></td></tr>
<tr><td>Totals</td><td></td><td></td><td></td></tr>
<tr><td colspan="4">School Improvement Goals</td></tr>
<tr><td colspan="4"></td></tr>
<tr><td colspan="4">What needs to be accomplished? How or what is needed to accomplish it?</td></tr>
<tr><td colspan="4"></td></tr>
<tr><td colspan="4">Mission/Vision Statement for Parent and Family Engagement This statement should align with school improvement goals</td></tr>
<tr><td colspan="4"></td></tr>
</table>

Template #2A - Evaluation current practices – School level

School Level - Evaluation of Current Practices

School checklist to evaluate the essential elements.

#1 Culture and climate - Checklist

Mission and Vision

- ☐ There is a mission/vision for family engagement.
- ☐ The statement is communicated to all stakeholders.

The school leader

- ☐ Endorses parent and family engagement and communicates the importance with staff.
- ☐ Shares the vision/mission for family-school partnerships.
- ☐ Provides opportunities to build staff's capacity to work in partnership with families
- ☐ Seeks staff's input on how to improve family-school partnerships.
- ☐ Engages with families and builds relationships with students and families.
- ☐ The principal or school leader Is visible on campus.

Campus

- ☐ The campus is family-friendly, welcoming to all families, and clean and attractive.
- ☐ The hallways display student work or projects.
- ☐ Staff is visible on campus.
- ☐ Diversity is recognized and embraced.
- ☐ New students and families to the school are offered a campus tour and provided a packet or handbook outlining the school's policies and procedures and contact information.
- ☐ There is signage directing families where to go on campus.
    - Signage is in multiple languages.
    - The front office is marked.
    - School hours are posted.
- ☐ There is adequate parking for visitors.
- ☐ There is an area (room, office space, bulletin board) where parents can access information and resources.
- ☐ There is a computer for parent use.

Front office

- ☐ Visitors are greeted as soon as they walk in the door.
- ☐ The counter has information relevant to parents and families.
- ☐ Phone calls are answered promptly and professionally

Page 2-School Evaluation of Current Practices

New students and families to the school are

- ☐ offered a campus tour
- ☐ provided a packet or handbook that outlines the school's policies and procedures along with contact information
- ☐ paired with a student/buddy
- ☐ paired with a mentor or staff member

Communication

- ☐ Parents have access to contact staff.
- ☐ Multiple forms of communication are utilized to get information to families.
- ☐ Information is provided in the family's native language.
- ☐ Communication is two-way, and there is a way for families to communicate with staff, ask questions, and share concerns.
- ☐ Multiple methods, including the use of technology, are utilized for communication.
- ☐ The school website is user-friendly and kept updated.
- ☐ The school website contains links and resources.
- ☐ Information that goes home to families is provided in an easy-to-read format free of educational jargon.

Opportunities

- ☐ Parents are aware of ways to be involved in their children's education.
- ☐ Flexible scheduling offers that the opportunities provided for parents are on different dates, times, locations, and avenues.
- ☐ Multiple opportunities are provided to families to get them engaged in their children's education and build relationships with staff.

Families can

- ☐ *visit campus*
- ☐ *participate in fun activities that allow time for building relationships with staff*
- ☐ *attend academic or informational meetings or activities*
- ☐ *volunteer*
- ☐ *be an advocate or have a voice in their child's education*
    - *SAC*
    - *PTO/PTA*
    - *parent committees*
- ☐ share questions/concerns
- ☐ give input through
    - evaluations
    - surveys

Page 3-School evaluation of current practices

Conferences

- ☐ There is a protocol for hosting parent-teacher conferences.
- ☐ Teachers follow a conference agenda and families have a copy of the agenda.
- ☐ Student data is shared during the conference.
- ☐ Families are allowed to share their concerns and ask questions.
- ☐ Educational goals are developed, discussed, reviewed.
- ☐ Parents leave the conference with something (examples; conference notes, resources, strategies, an educational plan, or goal).

#2 Challenges and Considerations

- ☐ Barriers that hinder engagement efforts are identified.

  Barriers are identified through
    - Data (school and student population and demographics)
    - Needs assessments or surveys
- ☐ Consideration is given to finding solutions to overcome barriers.

#3 Competency and Capacity

- ☐ Data is collected and reviewed to identify what staff and families need to work in partnership to support student achievement and success.

Staff

- ☐ Staff is provided learning through training, professional development, resources, or strategies to help them partner with parents.

Building capacity activities for staff are

- ☐ *planned with a purpose*
- ☐ *aligned with the mission/vision – goal*
- ☐ *support student achievement*
- ☐ *meet the needs of the staff*

Families

Building capacity activities for families

- ☐ align with the mission and vision for family-school partnerships
- ☐ support academic achievement
- ☐ meet the needs of the families
- ☐ provide information about how parents can monitor their child's progress and grades
- ☐ address the curriculum and State Standards
- ☐ inform parents about formal assessments or high stakes testing
- ☐ include student data and how to interpret the data
- ☐ offer skills or strategies for helping extend their children's learning outside the classroom

Now, from the information collected using the checklist – evaluate current programs and practices. What is working, and where are improvements needed?		
	+ what is working	**- improvements are needed**
#1 Welcoming families and building relationships		
Culture & Climate		
Communication		
#2 Identifying and addressing barriers that exist		
Staff		
Families		
#3 Opportunities to build capacity		
Families		
Staff		

Template #2B - Evaluation of current practices – Class/grade level.

Evaluation of Current Practices

Checklist for a Classroom, Grade Level or Department

#1 Culture and climate - Checklist

Mission and vision

- ☐ There is a school level mission and vision statement for family engagement.
- ☐ All stakeholders had buy-in on writing or revising the statement.
- ☐ The statement is communicated to all stakeholders.
- ☐ The statement is visible or in print.

Leadership

The school leader

- ☐ endorses efforts parent and family engagement.
- ☐ communicates the importance of engaging families in their children's education.
- ☐ provides opportunities to build staff's capacity to work in partnership with families.
- ☐ asks staff for their input on how to improve family-school partnerships

The campus

- ☐ The campus is family-friendly welcoming to all families.
- ☐ The campus is clean and attractive.
- ☐ The hallways display student work or projects.
- ☐ There is staff, including leadership, visible on campus.
- ☐ Diversity is recognized and embraced.
- ☐ There is signage (in multiple languages) directing families where to go on campus.
- ☐ Teacher names are posted on the outside of the classroom door
- ☐ Adequate parking is provided for visitors.
- ☐ There is an area (room, office space, bulletin board) with information and resources relevant to parents and families.
- ☐ A computer is available for parent use.

Front office

- ☐ Visitors are greeted as soon as they walk in the door.
- ☐ The counter has parent information.
- ☐ Phone calls are answered promptly and professionally.

Page 2 – Classroom evaluation of current practices

Classroom

- ☐ The classroom environment is conducive to all learning styles.
    - o Student work or projects are displayed.
    - o Seating arrangements allow for team building and collaboration.
    - o The environment is print-rich in subject and content.
- ☐ Students are welcomed and greeted when they enter and exit the room.
- ☐ Student successes are shared or celebrated.
- ☐ Expectations, rules, policies, and procedures are posted.
    - o Students know what is expected of them.
    - o Assignments are posted.
    - o All students are treated fairly.
    - o There is consistency with rules, procedures, and protocols.

Communication with families

- ☐ Parents have access to contact teachers and staff.
- ☐ Communication is two-way, and there is a way for families to communicate with staff, ask questions, and share concerns.
- ☐ Multiple forms of communication are utilized to get information to families.
- ☐ Technology is used for communication.
- ☐ Parents are informed or have access to what is happening in the classroom.
- ☐ Parents have a way of checking assignments or homework.

Communication to families includes

- ☐ newsletters
- ☐ calendars
- ☐ website, webpage
- ☐ social media or other technology app
- ☐ information is provided for non-English speaking families in their native language, and translation is provided when needed
- ☐ information on to monitor their children's progress
- ☐ classroom procedures, rules, policies, expectations
- ☐ Information is provided in an easy-to-read format free of educational jargon.

New students and families to the classroom are

- ☐ paired with a student/buddy
- ☐ provided information on the rules, policies, procedures, expectations

Opportunities provided to families

- ☐ Multiple opportunities are provided to families to get them engaged in their children's education and build relationships with staff.
- ☐ Parents are aware of ways they can be involved in their children's education.
- ☐ Flexible scheduling offers that the opportunities provided for parents are on different dates, times, locations, and avenues.

Page 3 – Classroom evaluation of current practices

Families are offered different types of opportunities:

- academic workshops to build families' capacity
- non-academic meetings and workshops
- informational meetings
- welcoming activities
- advocacy – parent committees

<u>Parent conferences</u>

- ☐ There is a protocol for hosting parent-teacher conferences
- ☐ Conferences
    - follow an agenda
    - share of data
    - take notes using a conference log or notes sheet that is given to parents to take home with them
    - allow parents a chance to discuss their concerns

<u>Ways to be involved</u>

Parents are aware of

- ☐ ways they can volunteer or help in the classroom,
- ☐ how they can share their specific skills or talents, and
- ☐ how they can be involved in their children's education at home.

#2 Challenges and Considerations

<u>The following information is known about students and their families</u>

- ☐ student population and demographics
    - family backgrounds
    - the language that is spoken in the home
    - siblings or younger children
    - work situation, schedules
    - educational level
    - culture
- ☐ student assessment data
    - areas students need additional help or remediation
- ☐ students and families are surveyed to find out what they need or want from the school

Through personal reflection determine if beliefs or perceptions have any bearing on:

- ☐ wanting or needing the support of student's families.
- ☐ recognizing the value in the contributions of families.
- ☐ appreciating, recognizing, or embracing diversity among students and families
- ☐ treating students and families fair and equal regardless of their culture, race, ethnicity, or background.

Page 4 – Classroom evaluation of current practices

Barriers or challenges

- ☐ Thought is given to barriers or challenges that hinder efforts to engage with families.
- ☐ Consideration is given to finding possible solutions to overcome barriers .

#3 Competency and Capacity

Teacher/staff capacity

- ☐ The principal has collected data to identify the needs of staff and families to work in partnership to support student achievement and success.
- ☐ The school provides knowledge (training, professional development), resources, and strategies to help you work in partnership with parents.

Staff need capacity building activities on the following:

- ☐ communication with families
- ☐ conferencing with families
- ☐ diversity
- ☐ culture
- ☐ subgroups
- ☐ teambuilding
- ☐ poverty
- ☐ building trust and relationships
- ☐ sharing data
- ☐ progress monitoring
- ☐ other:

Families need capacity building activities on the following:

- ☐ how they can monitor their child's progress and grades
- ☐ the curriculum and State Standards
- ☐ formal assessments or high stakes testing
- ☐ understanding student data
- ☐ skills or strategies of how to help extend their child's learning outside the classroom
- ☐ setting educational goals
- ☐ transitioning (ex: elementary to middle school, middle school to high school) college and career
- ☐ graduation requirements
- ☐ parenting skills
- ☐ literacy
- ☐ learning difficulties
- ☐ where to get resources or help
- ☐ connections with outside resources in the community

Page 5-Classroom evaluation of current practices

<u>Capacity building activities for families</u>

- ☐ are designed to meet a family need
- ☐ align with the mission and vision to support student achievement and success
- ☐ are offered in different formats depending on the best way to deliver the information
    - ○ meetings or workshops
    - ○ newsletters
    - ○ website or webpage
    - ○ resources
    - ○ other_____________

<u>What opportunities are offered to welcome families into the classroom?</u>

- ☐ orientation
- ☐ open house
- ☐ conferences
- ☐ other _______________

Evaluate your resources

Do not forget to look at all the available resources and funding sources. What is available and how are you utilizing them to support engagement efforts.

For example:

- *Human capital*
- *School funding*
- *Federal funding*
- *Grants*
- *Businesses and community partners*

The last step is to use this checklist to assess current practices. The next template is provided as a resource.

"Your ability to persevere in the face of adversity is what drives your success and achievements."

-Angela Duckworth

Now, use the checklist to assess current program and practices. What is working and where are improvements needed?		
	+ strengths	**- needs improvement**
#1 Culture and Climate – How welcoming is the culture and climate to families ? Is it conducive to building relationships? Is there effective, two-way ,communication?		
culture & climate		
communication		
#2 Challenges to Consider - Identify and address barriers		
school		
leadership or the school		
students		
families		
#3 Confidence and Capacity – What Opportunities to build capacity		
for teachers/staff		
for families		

Template #3A - Data collection sheet –School level

Data Collection Sheet School Level	
School **Academic School Year**	
School Improvement Goals	
Mission/Vision Statement for Parent and Family Engagement	
Goals	
Student Data	
# Students age/grade, gender	
sub-groups (Race, ethnicity)	
students with disabilities	
ELL/ESOL	
poverty (SES/F/RL%)	
Academic Data	
state assessment data	
other assessment data	

Page 2 – School level data collection sheet		
Data Trends		
Family/household data		
Needs-What does the data tell?		
School and staff needs	**Family needs**	**Student needs**

Identified barriers-based on needs and data collected		
	Barriers identified	**Possible solutions**
school		
staff		
families		
students		
other		

Other available supports	
funding sources	
business or community	
family talents skills	
other	

Template #3B - Data collection sheet –Classroom/ grade level

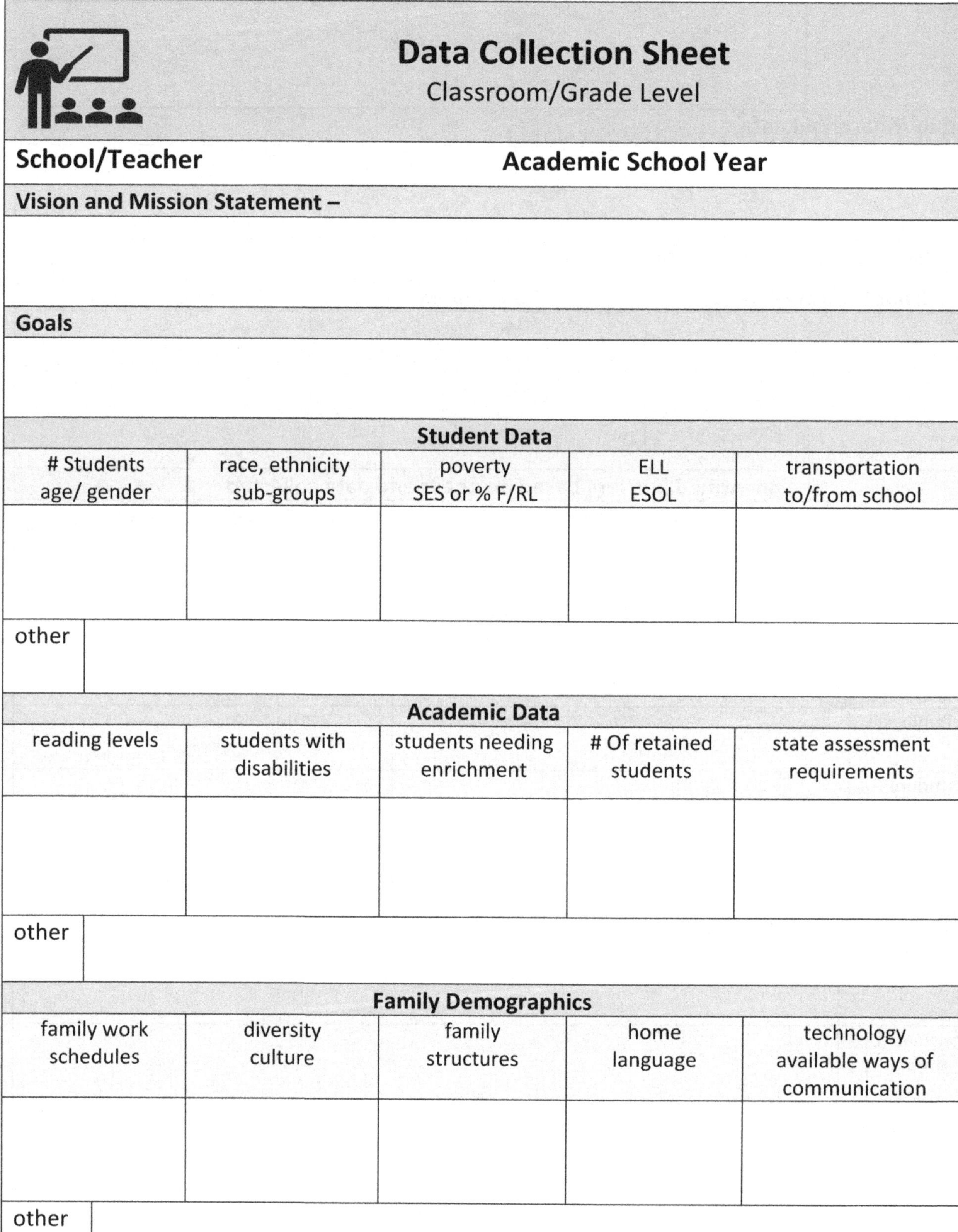

Data Collection Sheet

Classroom/Grade Level

School/Teacher **Academic School Year**

Vision and Mission Statement –

Goals

Student Data				
# Students age/ gender	race, ethnicity sub-groups	poverty SES or % F/RL	ELL ESOL	transportation to/from school
other				

Academic Data				
reading levels	students with disabilities	students needing enrichment	# Of retained students	state assessment requirements
other				

Family Demographics				
family work schedules	diversity culture	family structures	home language	technology available ways of communication
other				

Page 2 – Classroom data collection sheet

Identify Needs – **Review the student population and demographics data. What does the data tell?**	
Student Needs	**Family Needs**
Your needs	
Barriers - Based on the needs identified, which needs are barriers that hinder engagement? What are some possible solutions to overcome the barriers?	
barriers	
possible solutions	
Available support or resources (do not forget family skills/talents)	

Template #4A - Partnership plan-School level

School Level - Partnership Plan	
School:	Academic Year:
Mission/Vision	
family engagement team	
mission/vision statement	
goal(s) to accomplish	
Culture and Climate - What steps will be taken to improve the culture and climate?	
Welcome families and offer activities for families	
Make the school family-friendly	
Offer opportunities for relationship building	
Improve communication	
Ensure two-way communication	
Campus appearance	
Recognize diversity	
Create a safe learning environment	

Page 2 – School Partnership Plan	
#2 Challenges – What are barriers that hinder engagement	
Barrier	**Possible Solution**

Building Capacity Activities for Families - What types of activities (meetings, workshops, events) will be provided to families to build their competency and capacity for supporting their child's learning?

Academic – Based on the needs assessment

Who? Audience	**What?** Purpose - topic/subject	**When?**	**How?** format or delivery

Non-Academic – based on the needs assessment

Who? Audience	**What?** Purpose - topic/subject	**When?**	**How?** format or delivery

Page 3 – School Partnership Plan			
Informational – based on the needs assessment			
Who? Audience	**What?** Purpose - topic/subject	**When?**	**How?** format or delivery

What other supports are provided to families to build their capacity in	
Learning about the curriculum and standards	
How to have an effective conference with staff	
Understand state assessments and high stakes testing	
How to monitor their child's progress	
Ways they can be involved or volunteer	
How they can have a voice or be an advocate	
Learn about promotion or retention requirements	
Understand how to help their children transition between grades or school	
Understand graduation requirements	
How to help their child plan for college or a career	
other	

Page 4 – School Partnership Plan			
Build Capacity Activities for Staff			
Who? Audience	**What?** Purpose - topic/subject	**When?**	**How?** format or delivery

Roles and Responsibilities: (like a compact) To support student achievement and success, what is needed, who can help and how can they help?			
Need	**The school staff will:**	**The student will:**	**The family will:**

Template #4B – Partnership Plan – classroom, grade level, or department

Classroom - Partnership Plan

Note – adapt this to fit a classroom, grade level, or department

Have a goal for engaging families of the students in the classroom	
School's mission and vision for partnerships?	
What is the classroom goal for partnerships?	
Culture and Climate How does the classroom culture and climate support academic achievement and success? • What is done in each of these areas to support student achievement and success? • How are parents made aware? How can families support your efforts in each area?	
environment safety	
procedures	
rules & expectations	
organization and arrangement	
environment is print rich in content.	
celebrate student success	
class schedules	
classroom technology	
homework	
curriculum and assignments	
progress monitoring	
high stakes testing	
Communication with the teacher	

Page 2 – Classroom Partnership Plan	
Welcoming Activities - *Opportunities to visit the classroom*	
orientation	
open House	
Effective Communication	
Outgoing communication going home to families	
Type - Purpose	Method
Incoming communication coming from the home. ***How can parents:***	
ask questions	
share concerns	
Parent-Teacher Conference	
protocol	
schedule	
invitation	
agenda	
format	
data sharing	
conference log or notes	
follow - up	

Page 3 – Classroom Partnership Plan	
Identify and Address Barriers Be sure to review data	
Challenges	**Possible solutions**
language	
disabilities or accommodations	
family structures	
poverty	
parent's educational level	
availability of technology	
trust, beliefs, attitudes	

What support, funding, or resources are available?		
Family skills/talents	**Community or businesses**	**Funding/donations**

Template #5A - Plan a capacity building activity for families

Planning Sheet **Family Capacity-Building Activity**	
Topic	
Type of activity	____academic ______non-academic ______informational ______ other Does it align with student achievement? ______ Does it align with the mission/vision? ______ SIP goals?__________
Purpose of activity	
Audience or target group	
Anticipated (Time, date, location)	
Format or delivery	
Who is responsible? Or who is presenter?	
Family takeaway	
Materials or supplies	
Anticipated costs & Funds	
Anticipated barriers and solutions	____language ___transportation ____refreshments/food ___childcare or children's activities ____other____
How will parents be invited?	
Documentation	___invitation ___agenda/program ____sign in sheets ___evaluations ___other:________________________________
Helpers & assigned tasks	

Template #5B - Plan a capacity-building activity for staff

Planning Sheet

Staff Capacity-Building Activity

Topic	
Type of Activity	Does it support student achievement? _____ Does it align with the mission/vision for partnerships? ______ Does it align with school improvement goals? ____
Purpose of Activity	
Audience or target group	
Anticipated (Time, date, location)	
Format or Delivery	
Who is responsible? Presenter	
Materials or supplies	
Anticipated costs and funding	
How will staff be notified?	
Documentation	___invitation ___agenda/program ____sign in sheets ___evaluations
Helpers & assigned tasks	

About the author

Born and raised in Key West, Florida, Denise Diaz Atwell lives in Lakeland, Florida, with her husband, Everett. They have three grown children: daughters Alexa and Brooklynne (husband Billy) and son Corey. Atwell's career spans 30+ years in the K–12 public school setting. Her experiences include different teaching and administrative positions. More than half of Atwell's career has been working in or with Title I schools, including in 2011, when Atwell became the District Title I Coordinator for Parent and Family Engagement, monitoring 101 schools for compliance with Title I requirements until she retired in 2017.

Since retirement, Atwell has worked as a supervising professor with two local colleges in the education department to monitor and evaluate preservice teachers during field experience and final internship. Working with teacher candidates endorses the need for preparing new teachers to work in partnership with students and their families. In 2021, Atwell was hired, on contract, by the local public school system to monitor Title I private schools with Title I, II, and IV compliance, which includes a requirement for parent and family engagement.

Atwell's experience in public and private school settings and working at the college level with teacher candidates affirm the need for building educator capacity on the importance of parent and family engagement in education.

Education

Ed. D.	Doctor of Education—Curriculum and Instruction	Southeastern University
	Doctoral Coursework in Educational Leadership	Florida Southern College
M. S.	Master of Science—Educational Leadership	Nova Southeastern College
B. A.	Bachelor of Arts—Specific Learning Disabilities	University of South Florida

Certifications

Teaching Certificates

Educational Leadership K–12
SLD-Specific Learning Disabilities K–12
Elementary Education K–5
Early Childhood Education

Endorsements

ESOL-English for Speakers of Other Languages
Reading Endorsement K–12

National Board-Certified Teacher

Early Childhood Generalist-Certified in 1999

The author's research

The combined research included

1. a literature review of current literature and studies within the previous ten years on how schools build staff and families' capacity to support academic achievement and barriers schools face in family engagement,
2. a comparison study of research-based models for parent involvement,
3. a case study (Atwell, 2021), and
4. principal interviews conducted by Atwell (2019).

#1: A review of the current literature.

An extensive literature review about parent and family engagement in education uncovered the importance of allowing families to collaborate and make decisions about their children's education by creating family-school partnerships.

The review of the literature revealed the following:

- All parents want their children to succeed in school.
- Engaging families in their children's education is a protected right of parents by law.
- Parent and family engagement are a protected goal embedded in federal policy.
- Most educators
    - have a strong desire to work with families,
    - lack the skills and knowledge to engage with families,
    - struggle to cultivate relationships,
    - do not know how to form partnerships,
    - lack training for effectively working with diverse families, and
    - do not utilize research-based strategies or are aware of a model that supports efforts to build partnerships between home and school.
- Schools do not understand how to move engagement beyond getting parents to volunteer on campus.

Consistently, the literature revealed the following components are needed to sustain partnerships:

- Leadership is imperative to family-school partnerships and must communicate a joint mission and vision for family engagement.
- Establishing trusting relationships with students and their families is the first step toward forming partnerships.
- Identifying and addressing barriers that hinder engagement efforts is essential.
- Building the collective capacity of all stakeholders is needed to work in partnership.
- Identifying challenges to engagement exist for the school, the home, and the families, is imperative, but many educators are not trained to identify these challenges or address them."
- A common partnership goal must be supported by student learning, academic achievement, and school improvement.

#2: A review of research-based models for engagement

There are several research-based models or frameworks for parent and family engagement. Each model is founded on research-based principles, standards, or components and contains best practices, strategies, and conditions necessary for effectively engaging families in their children's education. See recommended resources.

Parent and family Engagement models

1. Joyce Epstein's Six Types of Parent Involvement
2. The National PTA Standards for Parent Involvement
3. Steve Constantino's Four Domains and Five Principles
4. The Dual Capacity-Building Framework for Family-School Partnerships

The findings

A broad comparison of the models revealed that many of the components overlap. The overlapping commonalities strengthen components necessary for effective parent and family engagement, such as communication, advocacy, or decision-making. Each of the four selected models shares the common goal of engaging families in their children's education and academic achievement. A comparison of the research-based models revealed overlapping commonalities as critical components for effective parent and family engagement.

The commonalities included

- effective (two-way) communication,
- building relationships,
- providing opportunities,
- building both staff and families' capacity to work together in support of student achievement or success,
- families' ability to advocate for their children, and
- identifying challenges that hinder engagement and finding ways to overcome the obstacles.

Comparing these research-based models and using my doctoral research led to ***The Essential Elements for Family-School Partnerships***.

- **Element #1** – The culture and climate of the school
- **Element #2** – Consideration of the challenges that hinder engagement
- **Element #3** – Build staff and families' capacity to partner in supporting student achievement.

To establish or sustain family-school partnerships, the elements must be addressed. Addressing the elements involves reviewing and analyzing data and developing a partnership plan.

#3: A case study

Atwell's (2021) dissertation "A Qualitative Case Study Exploring How Title I Schools Build the Capacity of Staff and Families to Support Academic Achievement" was a case study that explored family-school partnerships in five Title I elementary schools in one central Florida school district. The purpose was to discover how schools meet ESSA's Section 1116 compliance requirements to build staff and families' capacity to partner in school improvement and academic achievement.

More specifically, the study examined the opportunities schools provided to engage their students' families and how they built families' capacity to support and extend learning outside the classroom for their children. Additionally, the study examined how schools developed their staff's ability to work more effectively in partnership with parents to support student academics. The findings provided specific examples of capacity-building activities that schools extended to their staff and families. The results are presented in chapter 5

#4: Principal interviews

The case study only involved five elementary schools. Additional research was needed to understand what middle and high schools were doing to build staff and families' capacity, and interviews were conducted with four middle/high school principals.

The research questions

Case study questions

1. How do schools build the capacity of families to extend their children's learning beyond the classroom?

2. How do schools build staff capacity to partner with families to support student achievement?

Principal interview questions

1. How or what does your school do to build the capacity of families to extend their child's learning beyond the classroom?

2. How or what do you or your school do to build the staff's capacity to partner with families to support student achievement?

The findings

The findings are the data from the case study with five elementary schools and the principal interviews with four middle/high school principals.

The combined findings for Question 1

The data revealed that schools build their families' capacity in various ways, such as offering opportunities such as workshops, activities, or events and providing support through newsletters and on the school website.

1. ***hosting opportunities for families***
    - Opportunities included such as workshops, activities, or events
    - The purpose of these opportunities can be categorized as
        - academic or non-academic,
        - informational,
        - advocacy,
        - or welcoming activities that provide a means to build relationships.

2. ***providing other means of support to families***

Other supports, not considered an event or activity, provide parents with information, strategies, or tips through the website and in newsletters. Some topics included parenting tips and suggestions on homework and academics, progress monitoring, and communication.

The combined findings for Question 2

The combined data findings from the case study and the principal interviews revealed that schools provide training or professional development for their staff, which occurred through different formats and addressed various topics. Topics of staff capacity-building activities included communication, conferencing, diversity, data, student achievement and engagement, relationship building, team building, and cooperative learning.

Interestingly, schools varied in the format for capacity-building activities. Some schools used faculty meetings, grade-level meetings, or meetings by departments to have a building capacity activity. In contrast, other schools took advantage of the district's support by bringing in a guest speaker, having staff participate in district training, or utilizing resources such as PowerPoint presentations prepared by the district. Also discovered from the interviews was that principals ($n = 2$) mentioned team meetings when a student's needs are discussed to find ways to support that student's learning, which is considered a capacity building of their staff.

The Conclusion

From the research findings, Atwell (2021) concluded that effective parent and family engagement at the school and classroom level could be categorized into three essential elements: addressing the culture and climate, considering challenges, and building competence and capacity.

Recommended reading and resources

As educators, we all have a professional library or toolbox full of resources, mine included! Over the years, in both school-level and district-level positions, good fortune has allowed me to participate in many professional developments and conferences on parent and family engagement and collect resources on the subject. However, several publications became favorites and guided efforts in preparing presentations and training for teachers, principals, and parents and writing my dissertation.

Recommended publications.

Constantino, S. M. (2008). ***101 Ways to Create Real Family Engagement***. Engage Press. Galax, GA.

Constantino, S. M. (2016). ***Engage Every Family: Five Simple Princi****ples*. Corwin Press-A Sage Publication. Thousand Oaks, CA.

Epstein, J. L. (2001). ***School, Family, and Community Partnerships: Preparing Educators and Improving Schools.*** Westview Press. Boulder, CO.

Epstein, J. L., & Associates (2008). ***School, Family, and Community Partnerships: Your Handbook for Action***. *(Third Edition)*. Corwin Press. Thousand Oaks, CA.

Henderson, A. T., Mapp, K. L., Johnson, V. R., & Davies, D. (2007). ***Beyond the Bakesale: The Essential Guide for Family-School Partnerships***. The New Press. New York, NY.

Helpful online resources

Mapp, K. L., & Bergman, E. (2019). ***Dual Capacity-Building Framework for Family-School Partnerships*** (Version 2). SEDL. Retrieved from: www.dualcapacity.org

Mapp, K. L., & Kuttner, P. (2013). ***Partners in Education: A Dual Capacity-Building Framework for Family-School Partnership****s (Version 1)*. SEDL Retrieved from: https://www2.ed.gov/documents/family-community/partners-education.pdf

The National PTA Implementation Guide. Available from www.pta.org

The National PTA Standards for Parent Involvement. Retrieved from: https://www.pta.org/the-center-for-family-engagement

The author's dissertation

Atwell, Denise D., (2021). ***A Qualitative Case Study Exploring How Title I Schools Build the Capacity of Staff and Families in Support of Academic Achievement.*** (2021). Doctor of Education (E.D.). 80. Retrieved from .https://firescholars.seu.edu

Note from the author: *These recommendations are personal favorites, but by no means are they the only publications or resources available. As this journey continues, additional sources of information will be added to the toolbox. For disclosure purposes, there is no compensation of any kind for recommendations or endorsement of a publication.*

A successful parent a family engagement program

In 1998, the school I was teaching became a Title I school. I was offered a K–5 instructional support teacher position to monitor Title I compliance in our school. Part of Title I compliance was promoting parent and family engagement. Not knowing how to increase our efforts led to visiting several other Title I schools to beg and borrow ideas and learn how they got parents and families engaged. I developed a parent and family engagement program called "Global Learning through the Grades" with a team of teachers. The program was hugely successful, and attendance tripled at school events. In 2001, I received a Disney "Teacheriffic" special judges award with a Disney Mouseketeer trophy, $5,000 for me, and $1,500 for our school.

This program was a massive undertaking that involved buy-in from all the school staff. The project was a team effort and was most successful when those involved believed in our cause and supported the effort to host the events. Many staff volunteered their time, and the involved staff in each event were compensated or paid when appropriate.

We continued the theme "Global Learning through the Grades" for three consecutive school years until the theme had run its course. Then the program and monthly events were referred to as "Family Fun Nights." The family fun nights followed a similar agenda but a new theme for each event.

Another reason the events were successful is that each event offered something for every family. Our target audience for each event was the grade level performing, but many families attended the events even if their child was not performing. Topics for some parent workshops were repeated to offer families who missed the first chance to attend.

"The true sign of intelligence is not knowledge but imagination.
Imagination is everything.
It is the preview of life's coming attractions."
— Albert Einstein

An overview of the program

Global Learning through the Grades

A program to increase parent involvement

School: Title I elementary K–5

When: Every Month x 6 events
Time: 5:00 pm to 8 pm
Where: School Campus

Theme: A different country was highlighted each month, and a different grade level was performed.

Event Agenda

Time	Activities	Persons responsible
5:00 – 6:30 pm	• Meal in cafeteria • PTA snacks • Arts and crafts • Open library and computer lab • Community tables/exhibits	• Meals—cafeteria staff • PTA—snacks • Arts and crafts—volunteers • School librarian • Computer lab paraprofessional
6:30 – 7:15 pm	• Parent workshops (topics varied and repeated) • Children's activities • Childcare was provided	• Workshops and children's activities–volunteer staff • Childcare—Paid staff
7:15 – 8:00 pm	• Grade level performance representing a different country • Music and art shows represent a different country	• Performances—art and music teachers with the help of the grade level teachers

The reasons why this program was successful.

This program was successful for many reasons: teamwork, planning, communicating, inviting, evaluating, and encouraging.

There was a hook for getting families to attend

- **<u>dinner and student performances</u>**: Most parents want to see their children perform. Student performances got families to come on campus and encouraged families to participate in the other activities we offered. Along with student performances, we provided dinner at a reasonable price.

  Before the performances, we offered a variety of parent workshops and opened the media and computer labs for families to engage with their children in a non-threatening atmosphere.
- Part of our goal was to increase attendance at school events. The attendance at these events tripled from previous school-wide events. Our first step was to get families into the school and build relationships with them. Each event allowed us to embed workshops and activities into our schedule to build capacity. Every workshop provided parents with a takeaway to help them help their children.

The invitation was communicated in multiple ways.

- Parents received the dates of all activities at the start of the school year before each event, and families were reminded.
- Each event was advertised and marketed through flyers, the school website, on the school's marquee, in school and grade level newsletters, and with car pick-up and drop-off signs.

Barriers to participation were identified and addressed by

- translating for non-English-speaking families,
- offering food/dinner at a reasonable price,
- providing childcare and children's activities, and
- hosting various workshop topics gave parents a choice of what to attend based on their needs.

Families were welcomed

- **Staff circulated during the events** to meet and greet families and make them feel welcome.
- **Families were greeted** when they arrived and thanked when they left.
- The **administration was visible** on campus and opened the program or presentation with a word to families.

We offered incentives

- **Passports**—each family was given a ticket at the start of the school year. For each event families attended, they received a stamp on their passports.
- **Documentation (sign-in sheets)** was collected, and the classroom with the most attendance received a prize for providing a competitive spirit among classroom teachers and students.
- **Door prizes or giveaways** were held at the end of the event—this provided an incentive to families. We had the support of our PTA and local business partners to help with prizes.
- **Takeaways**—Title I funds allowed us to provide each child who attended a book to take home with their family. Title I fund also paid for materials or resources given to families.
- **Family photos** were taken at each event. Photos were posted on a family bulletin board and in our school newsletter (note...this was before the days of social media).

We reflected and evaluated to make the program better

- **Part of planning this program was surveying parents and** asking them what they wanted or needed from the school and staff.
- **Each event included an evaluation** asking families for feedback on what they liked about the event or where we needed to improve.

There was teamwork

This program took a team of people to make these events successful.

- **Leadership** attended each event.
- **Staff was on board**—volunteering their time, presenting at workshops, and helping with a variety of activities (academic and non-academic) for the children and families, such as opening the media center and computer lab for families to visit.
- **Teachers**—the art and music teachers were vital to developing student performances at each family night. In addition to the art and music teachers helping with the performance were also the classroom or grade-level teachers.
- **Community and businesses**—volunteered their time to do family presentations, held parent workshops, and donated materials or resources.

Most importantly, this program began with planning before the implementation. Having a well-developed plan for our program was our path to success! Planning involves collecting data and conducting needs assessments before developing a plan. Parents were given a calendar of dates at the beginning of the year. Invitations to each event were sent as the date got close, along with different reminders to market our events. After each event, we reviewed the data (evaluations and sign-in sheets) to reflect on how we could improve.

I hope you have enjoyed reading this book.
Keep making a difference in the lives of children.
Please take a moment to leave feedback
on Amazon.com.
Thank you!

Available from Amazon for $19.99
ISBN # 978-1-7374170-2-6

The Essential Elements of Family-School Partnerships

A resource for parents and families.

(Or anyone new to the field of education)

Made in United States
Orlando, FL
18 June 2024

47983920R00072